TAKING
PHOTOGRAPHS

Antoine Desilets

TAKING PHOTOGRAPHS

HABITEX BOOKS

- Cover Design by JACQUES DES ROSIERS
- Cover Photograph by ANTOINE DESILETS
- Interior Design and Layout by DONALD MORENCY
- English language translation and production supervision by:
  AMPERSAND PUBLISHING SERVICES INC., Toronto

Exclusive Distributor:
Collier-Macmillan Canada Ltd.
539 Collier-Macmillan Drive
Cambridge, Ontario N1R 5W9
Tel. (416) 449-7115 / (519) 621-2440

ISBN-0-88912-017-X

 2

Bibliothèque nationale du Québec
Dépôt légal — 3e trimestre 1974

Table of contents

(Photo by A.D.)

1 Has the increase in popularity of photography since World War II had any significant economic effects?

■■■■■■■■■■■■■■■■■■■■■■■■■■■■■■■■

There is no question that we live today in a kind of "golden age" of photography.

Although reliable statistics are difficult to obtain, some of the figures that **are** available are staggering. In the U.S. in 1971, for example, expenditures on all kinds of photographic equipment amounted to more than $4 billion. By comparison, this astronomical figure is as large as the entire budgets of some governments!

Other figures indicate that in North America, there are over 75 million cameras in circulation. This means that virtually one person in every three owns a camera of one kind or another.

The patterns in Europe and Japan are similar to those in North America. No figures are available, as far as I know, for the Soviet Union and most Communist bloc countries, although Czechoslovakia claims (in a recent article by Jean A. Keim) that " ... proportionate to its population, the number of cameras in this country exceeds that of the U.S., Japan and Germany and is the highest in the world"

Clearly, photography represents the foundation of very large and significant national and international industries. These industries employ literally thousands of people and generate turnovers in the billions of dollars.

In a real sense, the large-scale production of moderately priced photographic equipment in Japan after the war contributed to that country's economic recovery.

Moderately priced, high quality equipment also contributed largely to the popularity of photography during this period among young amateurs.

The development of new photographic materials — notably films and emulsions — and new processes has also had significant effects, as most owners of Polaroid cameras will agree.

All in all, photographic consumers provide a ready and willing market for a highly organized and skillful modern industry. Prospects for the decade ahead, moreover, appear to be almost as striking as the accomplishments of the one just past.

2 What should I know about light and colour temperature?

∎∎∎∎∎∎∎∎∎∎∎∎∎∎∎∎∎∎∎∎∎∎∎∎∎∎∎∎∎∎

Light and colour are identical. There is no colour without light and no light without colour; the slightest change in the quality of either light or colour will affect the quality of the other.

As a black element (like that on an electric stove) is heated, the light created by the heat changes from dark red to bright red and eventually through orange and yellow to white ("white-hot"). This colour is measured in degrees Kelvin (named after Lord Kelvin, the English physicist).

All colour emulsions are balanced for use over a very specific colour temperature range.

There are, therefore, three types of emulsion:

a) for daylight — 5900°K

b) for boosted artificial light (type A) — 3400°K

c) for non-boosted artificial light (type B) — 3200°K

It is essential to remember that the colour emulsion used must correspond to the colour temperature of the light being used.

It is also useful to remember that the lower the colour temperature of the light, the greater the proportion of reds (hot colour); and, conversely, the higher the colour temperature, the greater the proportion of blues (cold colour).

An ordinary lightbulb of	40 W is equivalent to 2750°K
An ordinary lightbulb of	60 W is equivalent to 2800°K
An ordinary lightbulb of	100 W is equivalent to 2850°K
An ordinary lightbulb of	500 W is equivalent to 2960°K
An ordinary lightbulb of	1000 W is equivalent to 3000°K
A projection lamp of	500 W is equivalent to 3200°K
Photofloods (boosted) of	250 W & 500 W are equivalent to 3400°K
Blue photofloods of	250 W & 500 W are equivalent to 5000°K
Daylight	is equivalent to 5900°K

Hot and Cold filters

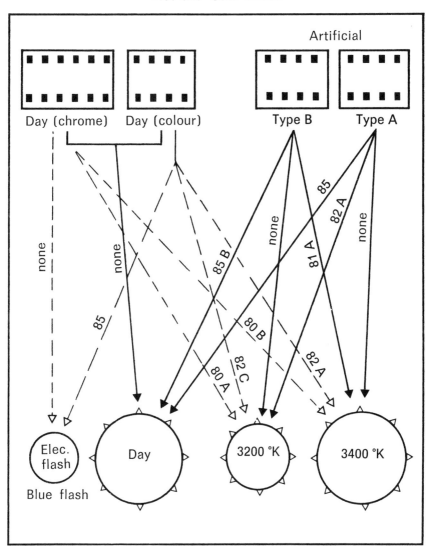

3 Can you give me a complete list of the 35mm black and white films most in use, along with their properties and prices?

■ I

There is little point in giving prices for film stock since prices are subject to change without notice from one week to the next.

The following list of films includes the best known brands available from professional suppliers of materials for the 35mm enthusiast. The choice available will allow you to try out several and make up your own mind.

You will notice in some cases two different sensitivity (ASA) figures for "day" and "indoors". This is because the film is more sensitive to blue and less sensitive to red. It is therefore necessary to take this into considera-

tion when taking a meter reading. As for the description of the graininess, it is valid as far as one can trust the manufacturers' own suggestions about handling the film in question. It should be noted that the lower the sensitivity figure, the finer the grain (this allows enlargements without the appearance of grain). Inversely, the higher this figure, the more pronounced the grain, even with only medium-sized enlargements.

For more details on graininess, contrast and density, I take the liberty of referring the reader to my earlier book, **Techniques of Photography.**

	ASA	Grain	Format
Panatomic-X	32	ultra-fine large blow ups	20-36 frame rolls 27-50-100 ft.
Plus-X Pan	125	medium general use	20-36 frame rolls 27½-50-100 ft.
TRI-X Pan	400	fairly good ideal for weak light	20-36 frame rolls 27½-50-100 ft.
2475 Recording Film	1000-1600	very grainy for fast shutter speeds in weak light	36 frame

High Speed Infrared	50 with red # 25 (A) filter	medium grain for penetrating atmospheric haze	20 frame 50-ft. rolls
High Contrast Copy Film # 5069	64 (int.)	ultra-fine for copying documents, etc.	36 frame 100-ft. rolls
Direct Positive Pan. Type 5326	80 (day) 64 (int.)	ultra-fine reversal	100-ft. roll (about $10)
ADOX KB-14	20 (day) 16 (int.)	ultra-fine general use	20-36 frame 50-ft. roll ($5)
ADOX KB-17	40 (day) 32 (int.)	very fine general use	20-36 frame 50-ft. rolls
ADOX KB-21	100 (day) 50 (int.)	fine general use	20-36 frame 50-ft. rolls

GAF

SuperHypan	500	medium grain weak light	100-ft. rolls 20 frame
Versapan	125 (day) 50 (int.)	fine grain general use	100-ft. rolls 20-36 frame

ILFORD

Pan F	50 (day) 40 (int.)	ultra-fine	20-36 frame
FP-4	125 (day) 100 (int.)	fine	20-36 frame
HP-4	400 (day) 320 (int.)	medium	20-36 frame

GEVAERT — AGFA

Iso-Pan-1FF	25	ultra-fine	20-36 frame
Iso-Pan-1F	80	fine	20-36 frame
Iso-Pan-155	200	fine	20-36 frame
Iso-Pan-Ultra	400	medium	

4

An expiry date appears on every box of film and printing paper. What happens if the film or paper is used after this date?

■ I

It must be emphasized at the outset that all photographic emulsions are subject to a process of aging or maturation, which is begun quite deliberately at the moment they are manufactured. It is this maturation which brings the film to a certain ASA level and which, depending on the treatment involved, gives us the specific figures of 10 to 400 ASA. This aging is therefore essential.

On the other hand, if film is not stored in a cool place — in a refrigerator or, better still, a freezer — the process of aging will go on, slowly but surely. Finally, after a certain period of time (generally two to three years), the emulsion turns into a sort of greyish fog, even before it is exposed to light. This process is speeded up *after the film has been exposed,* hence the manufacturers' w a r n i n g that films should be developed immediately after exposure.

Outdated colour emulsions are even more prone to an accelerated aging process than black and white emulsions. It is not advisable to buy colour film or paper which has expired. There will be a deterioration in the colour, accompanied by an overall bluish cast, lack of sparkle and an almost complete absence of saturation. An apple or tomato, by comparison, must be eaten when it has reached a certain maturity. Otherwise it will continue to ripen until eventually it will spoil. The same applies to colour emulsions.

It should be noted that Polaroid films are most vulnerable in this regard. Aside from the colorants they contain like any emulsion, they also carry their own developing agents which are very sensitive to heat and humidity.

When buying these films and papers, one can never be sure about the condition under which they have been stored. You can be certain, however, that retailers have no need to keep such supplies in the refrigerator. Demand is so high that they have no time to age on the shelf.

Outdated films and papers are becoming increasingly difficult to find. Problems arise more with the user who purchases a stock of films and papers and is then not careful to use them in the normal time.

I would hesitate to buy an outdated colour film (especially reversible slide emulsions), but would consider purchasing a negative colour emulsion or a black and white film, knowing that these permit certain corrections in the darkroom.

As for outdated printing papers, I would eagerly seek out a supply since they are often sold at half price. At the same time I would purchase a bottle of potassium bromide (a developer retarding agent). This chemical, which is used in the making of developers, slows down the action of developers on unexposed silver salts. By adding 15 or 20 grains of it to my developer, I can be sure that my outdated paper will have white, not grey, borders.

A loss of sensitivity is usually found in using outdated paper. The exposure must therefore be prolonged a few seconds.

Kodak produces an agent called Kodak Anti-Fog No. 1 which comes in both powder and tablet form and is added to the film or paper developer. It gives a marked improvement in the contrast of the photograph.

5 Is there some way of correcting, or at least improving, a badly underexposed colour slide?

Correction depends, of course, on the degree of underexposure. If the underexposure exceeds four stops, the slide must, for all practical purposes, be considered beyond repair.

I am speaking here of slides which have already been developed. (For those which have not, see "pushed" film, Question 6.)

If sufficient detail shows up when it is held in front of a strong light source, a duplicate slide incorporating the necessary corrections can be made.

It may be difficult to judge the correct exposure time. But if you know that the number of stops of underexposure is, say, three or four, a good starting point is to add that many stops to the original exposure.

Use a fairly high-contrast film, like Kodachrome II in daylight with electronic flash, or Kodachrome Type A with a 3400°K photoflood, or Ansochrome D-50 with electronic flash or daylight.

For greater convenience, and without spending too much, it is better to obtain a slide duplicator. This device is made precisely for producing a large number of duplicate slides. It allows you to work more systematically, in terms of focussing, the distance of the light source, the degree of magnification, etc. (See duplicates, Question 125.)

6 Is it possible to "push" a colour emulsion without adverse effects? Is this desirable?

■■■■■■■■■■■■■■■■■■■■■■■■■■■■■■■■■

It is certainly possible. As for being desirable, suffice to say that it can rescue a photographer who is faced with difficult lighting conditions.

Remember that any shooting done in conformity with the manufacturer's recommendations will give the best results. Changing the sensitivity rating of an emulsion (whether colour or black and white) is bound to alter the contrast and density balance of the emulsion, and this always results in colours which are not true.

The Kodak company suggests reluctantly that where it is absolutely necessary, you can double or even triple the rating of an emulsion (say of 125 ASA — Ektachrome type B), but they warn the photographer of a very marked increase in the contrast. The photographer will then be working at 250 or even 500 ASA, but he must develop the film according to the manufacturer's specifications, as follows:

Table of Adjustments for Pushed Ratings

Exposure	Ekta-chrome-X	Ektachrome High Speed (Daylight)	Ektachrome High Speed (Tungsten)	Developing time	
− 2 stops	250	640	500	Increase by	75%
− 1⅓ stops	160	400	320	" "	50%
− 1 stop	125	320	250	" "	35%
normal	64	160	125	Normal	
+ 1 stop	32	80	64	Decrease by	30%
+ 2 stops	16	40	32	" "	50%

(Photo by A.D.)►

7 Why do different colour emulsions produce a variety of results, and why is there not just one type of film?

Because the perception of colour varies so much from one individual to the next, there is a demand for many different types of colour emulsions. Manufacturers were quick to realize this and have made a wide range of colour film available to the consumer. Selecting one in particular often becomes very difficult. Here are a few comments on the colour films most in use:

1. Kodachrome II, 35mm slide format, and Kodachrome X:

a) Kodachrome X, Kodachrome II and type A can only be developed by the Kodak laboratories. The cost of developing is included in the purchase price.

b) They are available in cartridges and in 35mm rolls of both 20 and 36 frames.

c) Ideal films for those who want saturated, even loud, colour, they give slightly more contrast than other films, which means a sharper picture.

d) Kodachrome II and Kodachrome X (25 ASA and 64 ASA) for daylight may be used with surprisingly good results indoors, providing a conversion filter is used (80 A or 80 B, depending on the lighting — see instructions).

e) Kodachrome permits a greater exposure latitude than Ektachrome, in the sense that it has a better tolerance for pushed exposures.

f) Their grain (or any appearance of grain) is practically nonexistent.

g) They are perfectly balanced for magnesium and electronic flash (II and X).

h) The "A" types are balanced for artificial light of 3400°K, 40 ASA without filter, and 3200°K, 32 ASA, with an 82A filter. They may also be used outdoors with the 85 filter at 25 ASA.

2. Ektachrome X:

a) A remarkable film for shooting slides under all conditions. Medium fast 64 ASA available in both 20- and 36-frame rolls, 127-120-620-828.

b) Ideal for capturing pastel hues. Colour rendering is excellent under a cloudy sky or in the shade.

c) This film has become popular with the public, for it responds well in situations where lighting conditions are difficult to estimate as in the presence of lamps or fluorescent bulbs.

d) Another advantage in the use of this film (as well as the High Speed Ektachromes) — when lighting is poor, is that it can be pushed to 2½ times its ordinary speed. In the case of Ektachrome X, the speed would be 160 ASA instead of 64, but it must be developed with the Ektachrome Special Processing kit (ESP-1). This will provide more than acceptable results.

e) Note, however, that no emulsion will give the best results unless exposed in accordance with the manufacturer's specifications. This applies to all colour films.

f) As Ektachrome X is less contrasty than Kodachrome, it gives the **impression** that photos are less sharp. On the screen, this slight difference will go unnoticed by the majority of viewers.

3. High Speed Ektachrome (Improved Daylight):

a) This is a very fast film which appears at first to give only moderate colour saturation. It reacts particularly well to pushing, even as far as 500 ASA. This feature puts it in the same range as black and white film, and permits shooting with available light and shutter speeds that don't necessitate the use of a tripod. Action photos become possible without flash.

b) This film is competently backed up by its twin, type B for artificial light (3200°K — 125 ASA). These two emulsions finally made it possible to shoot indoors without flash. With an average shutter speed of 1/30 sec. at f/2.8, you can shoot almost anywhere inside a well-lit house.

c) Both may be used either indoors or outdoors with the aid of an appropriate filter: type B outdoors with an 85B; the daylight type indoors with an 80A or 80B, depending on the kind of lighting.

d) The grain in these emulsions is a little more evident than in Ektachrome X, but it scarcely shows if viewing is done from a respectable distance. (See Question 14 on Anscochrome 500.)

8 What are the advantages and disadvantages of the ultra-rapid film called Kodak Recording 2475?

Press photographers frequently use this film when they must work in places which are poorly lit, or where the use of flash is forbidden or inappropriate.

The film's sensitivity, according to Kodak, is 1000 ASA. This is its normal rating (developer DK-50, 5 min. at 68°F., but it is often pushed to 4000 ASA (37 DIN).

At this very high rating, it must be processed in a powerful developer, Kodak DK-50, freshly mixed from a pure supply, 8-10 min., at 68°-70°F.

Such high panchromatic sensitivity automatically makes it a high-grain film, but you will have good results if the correct developing method is followed. Attention must be paid to the type of developer and its temperature, as well as the drying temperature, which must not be too high. (See the instructions which come with the film.)

Another advantage of this film is the estar base on which the emulsion is laid. The base is thinner, more durable, and practically impossible to tear with the fingers (which is not true of other types of film). Moreover, this base offers better anti-halo protection.

Even at 3000 ASA the grain is acceptable

My favourite cook. Kodak Recording 2475 at 2000 ASA — 1/250 sec. at f/8'

9 Can Ektachrome Infrared film be used as easily as other colour films?

■ ■

Originally conceived for wartime use (to detect certain kinds of camouflage), Kodak Ektachrome Infrared film is now very popular among both amateurs and professionals who want to add another dimension to photography's creative possibilities.

Its colour rendering is completely false. Contrary to the traditional colour films, which are sensitive to blue, green and red, this film, which is generally used with a Kodak Wratten #12 filter, is more sensitive to green, red and infrared radiation. Its sensitivity rating is 100 ASA.

Results with it are rather unpredictable. You should therefore do a few tests with different filters. It must however be exposed under lighting conditions with the same characteristics as daylight.

As far as processing is concerned, infrared film responds equally well to the usual E2, E3 or E4.

This film is so sensitive to infrared radiations that it must be loaded in total darkness.

If you do not do the processing yourself, you must warn the commercial lab what kind of film it is. It should always be kept in its own metal box. Special precautions must be taken when processing infrared film.

See colour plate 3

(Photo by A.D.) ➤

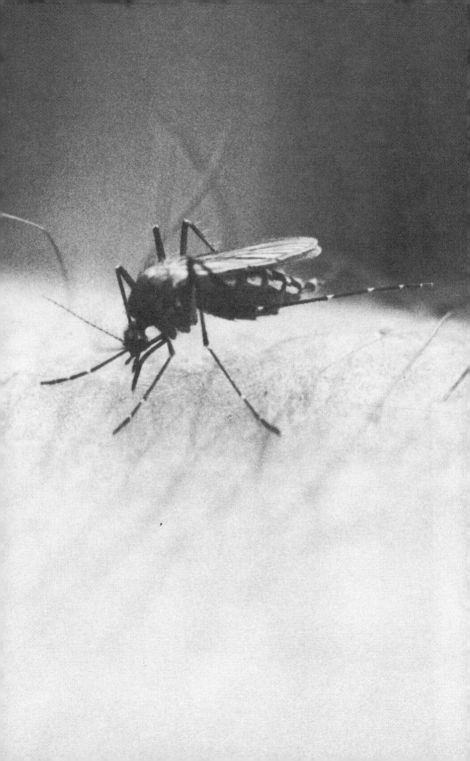

10

In order to make a black and white negative from a colour slide (for printing black and white proofs), what film should I use?

■ ■

A simple solution is to photograph your scene on black and white film, just as you would have done with your camera in the first place.

The scene (slide) to be photographed can now be corrected with the help of a yellow, green or red filter, depending on whether you want to bring out, or play down, certain grey tones.

Since we are dealing with a colour scene which is to be transposed into a continuous spectrum of greys, we must use a panchromatic emulsion, that is, one which is sensitive to all colours.

This method of reproduction always results in a negative which is too contrasty when processed according to the classical procedure.

Furthermore, a very fine-grain emulsion must be used, because we are shooting a "picture" (emulsion) which already has grain.

Since Tri-X is fairly grainy and Panatomic-X produces too much contrast, I would suggest using Kodak's Ektapan. It is the perfect compromise; it is medium-fast and offers medium contrast with excellent grain. An alternative compromise would be to use Kodak's Professional Copy Film which is sold in 4 x 5 in. sheets. This is a very convenient format, because it is fairly large. There are other sizes to choose from as well, starting with the 8 x 10 in.

One of the advantages of this method of reproduction is that it allows you to crop the original scene.

First Method — The slide is inserted in the enlarger (like regular black and white film). The image is focussed on the aligner.

The projected image will be in colour, as we would see it on a projection screen.

The projection "light quality" is of no importance, since the reproduction is going to be in black and white. What is important is that it not be too strong. A 211 bulb should be used.

Because Ektapan film is much more sensitive than ordinary enlarging paper, you might be tempted to stop right down to f/22, but I would advise that you do not go beyond f/8 (see Question 45), in order to maximize the resolving power of the lens.

What this means, of course, is an exposure time which is too fast to be practicable, hence the necessity for a 2X neutral density filter and the use of a test strip. To avoid excessive contrast, overexpose a little and develop slightly less.

Second Method — Use a slide duplicator, which, as its name indicates, is used to reproduce slides.

Developing can be done with Microdol X diluted 1 to 3, or D76 diluted 1 to 1. Naturally this latter method does not allow for any correction of lights and darks, as is the case with the enlarger method.

(Photo by A.D.)

11

If the colour temperature of a sunrise or sunset is between 2000° K and 3200° K, should I use a type B emulsion?

The manufacturers of photographic emulsions warn photographers about changes in the quality of light in the hours preceeding or following sunrise, for the obvious reason that their products are balanced for a colour temperature of around 5900°K to 6000°K.

The colour temperature of the rising sun is about the same as that of the setting sun, that is, "hot". One can, in theory, use a type B emulsion (balanced for hotter colour temperatures — 3200°K), but it is not easy to find the exact moment when this colour temperature has been reached.

Colour temperature changes very rapidly by a good many °K per hour from morning through late afternoon; the colour temperature at "high noon" is usually about 6000°K.

Given these difficulties, I think it is better to use a daylight film. This usually means adding a blue Kodak 82A or 82B filter to make the necessary corrections in the red colour cast, especially in the case of close-up portraits. The 82A and 82B filters are "cooling" filters, which serve to attenuate a red colour cast without affecting the other colours. (See Question 2)

See colour plate 5

(Photo by A.D.) ➤

12 Is there a colour film which can be exposed in ordinary household light (40, 60 or 100 watts) and which is capable of giving good colour rendering?

No! The manufacturers produce only two kinds of colour emulsion, type A and type B.

Type B films are made especially for artificial lighting in general, which means they can be used with 250, 500 or 1000 W lamps whose colour temperature is from 2900°K to 3200°K.

The type A films are balanced for boosted lighting of 3400°K. For example Kodachrome II, type A, 40 ASA.

Type B is therefore ideal for shooting indoors without special lighting. A film balanced for a colour temperature of 2800°K (which corresponds to 40, 60 and 100 W bulbs) would not be of much use, since you want to preserve the ambience of your subject in the photograph. Type B gives excellent results. Its slightly hot colour rendering has a very pleasant quality and marks a photo taken without filter in available light. You will have no doubt noticed some magazines which use photographs with a distinct reddish cast (typical of feature-article photography).

On the other hand, if you must re-balance your light by cooling it somewhat, you have only to use a correction filter, either 82A, 82B or 82C, which is dark blue. You will manage one way or another to push the colour temperature to 3200°K, but at the price of an exposure surplus of $2/3$ to 1 full stop. This, unfortunately, reduces your sensitivity rating by 50%, and also destroys the "available lighting" ambience. Since indoor lighting conditions are always poor, a fast emulsion (125 ASA) is obviously necessary. It will drop to 75 ASA if you use an 82C filter.

See colour plate 6

(Photo by A.D.)➤

13 For travel and other general purpose photography is it better to use negative colour film or slide film?

■ I

Personally, I prefer negative film for several reasons. First of all, I do not like to subject my guests to long evenings of viewing slides I have taken on my last holiday trip. Therefore, I really have little use for slide films.

I think of colour negative film as a "universal" film. I find that its advantages outweigh its disadvantages. It affords an opportunity to print photos of any size, as well as to crop a badly framed shot when necessary. You can also print black and white pictures with ease and make any necessary corrections. Furthermore, it allows for adjustments in the colour balance (density, contrast). Finally, any number of slides can be made from colour negatives.

The only disadvantage is the difficulty in reading colours when the negative is held against the light.

As far as slides are concerned, they cannot be viewed and appreciated without the aid of a magnifying glass or a projector.

admit that, when projected, slide film does give a more brilliant colour range than colour negatives. Kodachrome, for example, has this fine brilliant quality and good colour saturation. On the other hand, it is practically impossible to correct shooting errors. You must have an internegative made in order to get colour or black and white prints, and this procedure involves considerable loss of quality.

All in all, I prefer to have a colour print, however beautiful a slide may be when projected. However, the choice is yours. The purchase price of the slide is higher, but all-inclusive. The cost of the colour negative, while slightly lower when purchased, does not include the cost of running off prints.

See colour plate 1

(Photo by A.D.)►

14 Does Anscochrome 500 live up to its good reputation? What happens when it is pushed to 1000 ASA?

Yes, Anscochrome 500 is a real performer! The Gaf Company has perfected a colour emulsion for daylight which is more sensitive, or faster if you like, than Kodak's black and white Tri-X (400 ASA).

Surprisingly, Anscochrome 500 does not produce the coarse grain typical of other fast films. The grain is no more apparent than that produced by Anscochrome 200.

When Anscochrome 500 is pushed to 1000 ASA there is no real problem except for the grain. However, it is necessary to process it at least 17 minutes in the first developer, as opposed to the usual 8½ minutes (at 80°F) as well as to tone down the blacks.

Keeping in mind that the Anscochrome emulsions of 50 and 100 ASA offer much more latitude and greater definition, it is quite feasible to take action shots at 1/1000 sec. and f/11, in full sunlight, with a colour saturation which will compare favourably with Kodak's "chromes".

For those of you who really like grain, I suggest pushing it to 2000 ASA. This will give you everything you have ever wanted in grain. Your slides will look a bit unreal, and the colours quite unnatural, but what fantastic grain!

It is possible to use Anscochrome 500 simply as is, with tungsten lighting, but reds will dominate. On the other hand, you will get excellent results by using an 80 A filter and reducing the sensitivity rating to 125 ASA. I consider Anscochrome 500 to be a real break-through, perhaps the most important in colour emulsions in the last decade. Try it for yourself and see what you think!

See colour plate 8

(Photo by A.D.)►

15 Is it possible that copies made from the new Ektachrome duplicating film are absolutely identical to the original?

■ I

To say that the copies or duplicates are absolutely identical to the original is perhaps a slight exaggeration. It is safe to say, however, that of all the emulsions designed to produce a perfect copy of the original, the new Ektachrome Duplicating Film 6120 by Kodak is without doubt the best.

The reproduction of slides has always presented the problem of excessive contrast which was impossible to balance. If you overexposed and underdeveloped you could get some correction, but always at the expense of the colour rendering.

With this new copying film, there is a considerable lowering of contrast. It obviates the use of a contrast reducing screen, to which professionals often had to resort when using the older emulsions.

Now, professional photographers can store their precious originals in a file and submit the copy to a client. There is also the great advantage of being able to crop an original which otherwise may have been considered wasted.

The reproduction is carried out exactly as for the enlarging of a colour negative. Apart from any improvement in the framing, the slide can be made lighter or darker. When enlarging, any necessary colour corrections are made with compensating filters.

The 6120 duplicating film is well matched with Ektachrome E3 in the processing stage. Just remember to process longer in the first developer, and agitate more briskly.

The recommended lighting must have a colour temperature of 3200°K. Use of electronic flash is not recommended, however, in order to avoid the reciprocity problem.

See colour plate 7

16 What is meant by the "storage power" of an emulsion?

All photographic emulsions are made with a silver salt compound which is light-sensitive. Once developed, the emulsion may darken to the point of being opaque.

Both black and white and colour emulsions turn black according to the intensity and length of exposure to a light source.

Do not confuse the density of the film with contrast. The ability of a light-sensitive surface to "store" light is a reminder of a basic rule of photography; the exposure time affects the density, while the developing time affects the contrast.

If a photograph is exposed long enough, a moonlit scene can easily be transformed into one as bright as day, or even over-exposed.

This procedure is very common in astronomy, where very long exposure times (hours or even days) are used to photograph stars which are many light-years away.

Note also that prolonged development of a film accentuates contrast. It becomes fairly easy to balance the range of lights and darks by playing with exposure and development times.

At Montreal airport, the plane taking the exiled kidnappers to Cuba. Fast exposure — ¼ sec. at f/28. ➤

Same camera, a few minutes later, but with a longer exposure — 4 min. at f/4. Even in total darkness you can get an overexposure if you want. ➤

The
Andromeda
galaxy

17 Is it true that there is a safety margin in the sensitivity ratings of black and white films?

Although the manufacturers will not publicly acknowledge this, it is a known fact that a safety margin exists. It is important protection for amateur photographers who work in black and white.

Here is an example of what it means. The sensitivity rating of Tri-X film is stated as 400 ASA, whereas in reality it is closer to 650 ASA.

As we know, if a black and white film is exposed according to a rating of 400 ASA, although it is really 650, then it will be slightly overexposed ... by about 1/3 to 1/2 stop.

A film which is slightly over-exposed is always greatly preferable to one which is under-exposed. In the latter case, any shortcoming in the film, such as a lack of detail in the shadows, cannot be compensated for in the printing process. Overexposure, on the other hand, guarantees a surplus of detail in the shadows. This is easier to work with since the contrast can be adjusted during printing by using a softer paper.

Photo shot at 1600 ASA — standard development (as if for 400 ASA). ➤ There is a marked absence of detail in the shadows, even when printed on soft paper.

The same shot at 1600 ASA, but developed for twice the normal time. There is a little ➤ more detail in the shadows, and much better over-all contrast.

This time it was shot at 650 ASA and developed ➤ normally (as directed). On the whole very acceptable.

18 What are the comparative sensitivity ratings for ASA (American), DIN (German), GOST (Russian), Weston, and Scheiner ?

■ I

By way of explanation of the two most popular ratings, ASA stands for American Standards Association, and DIN stands for Deutsche Industries Norm. The chart below shows the comparative sensitivity ratings.

Light Pyrotechnics: ➤

ASA	DIN	GOST	WESTON	SCHEINER
6	9/10	12	5	29
8	10/10	16	6	20
10	11/10	20	8	21
12	12/12	25	10	22
16	13/10	32	12	23
20	14/10	40	16	24
25	15/10	50	20	25
32	16/10	65	24	26
40	17/10	80	32	27
50	18/10	100	40	28
64	19/10	125	50	29
80	20/10	160	64	30
100	21/10	200	80	31
125	22/10	230	100	32
160	23/10	320	125	33
200	24/10	400	160	34
250	25/10	500	200	35
320	26/10	650	250	36
400	27/10	800	320	37
500	28/10	1000	400	38
650	29/10	1250	500	39
800	30/10	1600	650	40
1000	31/10	2000	800	41
1300	32/10	2500	1000	42
1600	33/10	3000	1300	43

19 What are the principal characteristics of black and white infrared emulsions?

■ ■

The infrared emulsions were originally developed for scientific use, such as aerial, medical and forensic photography.

Many amateurs and professionals now use them when they want to create bizarre or surrealistic special effects, in colour as well as black and white.

Black and white infrared film is sold at all photographic dealers and suppliers. Ektachrome Infrared (colour) is a little more difficult to find. (See Question 9)

Its price is about the same as that of panchromatic emulsions.

Because this film is extremely sensitive to infrared radiations, it should be loaded and unloaded in a dark place, totally dark if possible. It should always be kept in the little metal box it is sold in until developing. If you do not do your own developing, be sure to warn the commercial lab that you are sending infrared film.

Modern cameras have a little red dot on the focussing ring to indicate the adjustment which has to be made for infrared film. Infrared radiations are longer than visible radiations and are not refracted in exactly the same plane. The correction corresponds to approximately 1/200 of the focal length. (This applies only to black and white infrared film.)

Manufacturers do not give any particular sensitivity rating, but simply recommend an exposure time of about 1/25 sec. at f/8 for landscapes, with a Wratten A #25 filter (red of course) which equals roughly 50 ASA in the sun.

If the manufacturers are vague about the sensitivity rating, it is simply to assure the photographer safer results. Because light meters react only to visible radiations, and not to infrared radiations, using a meter would be bound to give a false exposure.

The manufacturers therefore recommend using a tripod for a subject which is close up: the shutter can be held for 1/2 sec. at f/22. Stopping down in this manner will assure a sharper image and thereby compensate for focussing difficulties which tend to be more serious with infrared film.

Developing is as usual, with Microdol or D-76, following the manufacturer's directions.

It is important with infrared film to "triple up" on your shots. That is, shoot one exposure according to directions, then another underexposed one stop and a third overexposed one stop. Above all, work only in clear, sunny weather.

Infrared film with a # 25
Wratten A filter —
1/4 sec. at f/16 with tripod

Kodak infrared film with # 25
Wratten A filter —
1/4 sec. at f/16

20 Is it true that refrigerating colour and black and white film will put a halt to the aging process for an indefinite period of time?

In order to understand the aging process of film you must first know how a photographic emulsion is made.

A colour emulsion is made up of couplers which contain a colorant base. These colorants undergo significant changes over a period of time; the way in which film is stored greatly affects these changes.

Humidity and heat are, without doubt, an emulsion's worst enemies.

It is strongly recommend that any film stock not in current use be stored in a refrigerator at a temperature of less than 50°F. The process of deterioration begins at a temperature of 75°, and in humidity greater than 50%.

Many photographers **freeze** their film, especially if they have been able to acquire a large quantity of stock from the same lot. This assures them of a steady supply over a long period of time, without the problem of slight variations from one lot to the next.

Film must be stored **unopened** in its original container. Otherwise it will not be protected against humidity.

The same rule applies to rolls of exposed film which you might want to store and develop all at once. This assures uniform treatment in the one mixture of chemicals.

Any film which is kept frozen between 0°F. and −10°F. (for quite some time, even as long as several years), will not undergo any serious deterioration of its colorants.

If a film has been stored at a temperature of less than 50°F. it must be left out at room temperature for an hour before being loaded in the camera.

If it has been frozen, it should be allowed to warm up for three hours before use.

In either case, do not remove the film from its aluminum foil wrapping while it is warming up.

**My film stock occupies
a privileged place
in the freezer**

21 What are the true primary colours: blue, green and red; or blue, yellow and red? (Additive colour synthesis)

This question underlines the confusion which exists in the minds of many people who actually work with colour every day, in schools of art and in the printing industry.

The only way to clear this up is to begin by looking at how colour is related to light.

It may be a truism, but it can never be repeated too often: **it is light which produces colour and not material objects.** In order for there to be a sensation of colour, there must be: (1) an emitter (light source) and (2) a receiver (eye). If the eye is looking directly at an electric lamp, it will see only white light, devoid of any colour. Nevertheless, if a glass prism is placed in the path of the light rays (this is what happens with a rainbow) and the light leaving the prism is focussed on a screen, you will see the colours which comprise the visible spectrum.

We know that light is composed of electromagnetic waves of different lengths. The particular colour which the eye perceives is a function of the wavelength of the light which strikes the retina. Thus a wave 450 nano-metres in length (1 nm = 1 millionth of a millimetre) will produce the sensation of blue in the eye. The visible spectrum ranges from 400 to 700 nm, and a different colour is associated with each wavelength.

You can easily see how a mixture of different wavelengths, not to mention of different intensities, can yield an infinite variety of hues and nuances of colour.

A great variety of colour can be obtained by modulating only three basic colour "signals", blue, green and red. This is what is known as the **trichromatic effect** or additive colour synthesis. These three colours which are capable of producing any imaginable hue, including white, are called the primary colours.

Furthermore, when you mix two primary colours in a certain way, you create a **secondary colour,** as follows:

blue + green = cyan (blueish green)
blue + red = magenta (purple)
green + red = yellow.

(Photo by R.W.)

22 If the true primary colours are blue, green and red, why do colour emulsions contain layers of yellow, magenta and cyan? (Subtractive colour synthesis)

If two or three primary colour **pigments** are superimposed, the result will be a dark, almost black, tint. To understand this, we must first understand how the colours of **material objects** are perceived. Let us repeat once again that colour is produced by the light which falls on objects, rather than by the objects themselves. One could say in fact that objects have no colour as such. However, the **pigments** with which they are covered have a certain molecular structure which **selectively absorbs** light waves of a particular length, and **reflects** others. Thus, a lemon appears yellow in ordinary light because the molecular structure of its skin absorbs most of the blue radiations and reflects the green and red radiations. When the green and red radiations reach the retina of the eye, they produce a sensation of colour which is interpreted by the brain as yellow (green + red = yellow).

But now let us light the lemon with a source which gives off only green radiations. The green light will be reflected towards the eye by the surface pigment of the lemon and the lemon will appear to be green. By the same principle, it will seem red if the light falling on it contains only red radiations.

See colour plate 9

(Photo by R.W.)

23 Why does one speak of "colour temperature" in relation to photographic light sources?

■■■■■■■■■■■■■■■■■■■■■■■■■■■■■■■

When a metal filament is slowly heated, it emits a reddish light which becomes brighter as the temperature rises (wavelength ranging from 700 to 600 nm). As the temperature climbs higher still, the light turns yellow: green radiations (wavelength ranging from 600 to 500 nm) are now added to the red radiations and, as we know from the principle of additive synthesis, red light plus green light equals yellow light.

If the temperature continues to go up, blue radiations (500 to 400 nm) will appear and, in combination with the others, will give us white light. This is how the notion of temperature becomes associated with that of colour in physics.

Physicists have constructed a reference scale between a so-called "black body" and the **quality** of emitted light, that is, its spectral composition. The temperature is expressed in **degrees Kelvin,** units of the Kelvin scale or scale of absolute temperatures.

It is important for the photographer to know the colour temperature of a light source because the colour temperature indicates the relationship that exists among the primary radiations in the light source — blue, green and red; or, more simply, which is the **dominant.**

What is termed **white** light in physics is essentially neutral or **achromatic,** since it contains 1/3 of each of the primary colours. It contains no dominant. Its colour temperature is 5400°K. Sunlight is a good example of white light.

When the colour temperature diminishes, the percentage of blue radiation falls off, and the dominant tends towards yellow, then orange. On the other hand, when the colour temperature goes above 5400°K., the dominant becomes blue. Daylight, which is the product of **both** the sun and a blue sky, has a colour temperature of 6000°K.

Moreover, since colour emulsions are balanced for three precise kinds of light (6000°K – daylight type, 3400°K – type A, 3200°K – type B), an understanding of the notion of colour temperature gives the photographer total control over the quality of his product. Specifically, it allows him:

a) to choose the type of film appropriate to the lighting being used,

b) to compare two light sources. (For example, a photoflood bulb [3400°K] gives off a light which is less yellow and therefore more blue, than a 3200°K. photographic lamp.)

c) to predict what the false colour cast or dominant hue will be when the lighting is inappropriate. (For example, a type B [3200°K] emulsion used with household lighting [about 2800°K] will give slightly "hotter" rendering than normal.)

d) to choose the filter which will correct any lighting whose colour temperature is not appropriate. For example, light coming exclusively from a blue sky has a colour temperature of around 10,000°K; daylight (sun and sky together) registers about 6000°K. Even a daylight-type emulsion will give a false bluish cast in this case. To obtain a more natural colour rendering, you must use a filter which will absorb the excess blue, that is, a yellowish filter (filter series 81).

See colour plate 10

The Kelvin Scale

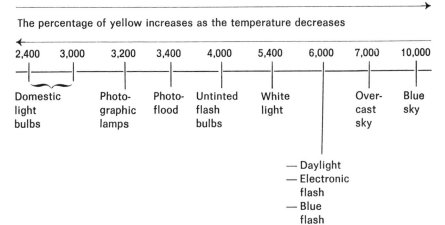

The percentage of blue increases with the colour temperature

The percentage of yellow increases as the temperature decreases

| 2,400 | 3,000 | 3,200 | 3,400 | 4,000 | 5,400 | 6,000 | 7,000 | 10,000 |

Domestic light bulbs

Photographic lamps

Photoflood

Untinted flash bulbs

White light

Overcast sky

Blue sky

— Daylight
— Electronic flash
— Blue flash

24 What general characteristics do compensating, correction and conversion filters have in common?

These filters are all used in colour photography (shooting and/or printing).

In one way or another, they all affect the "quality" or "spectral composition" of the light which strikes the film, and thus permit a measure of control over the final tint of the colour slide or print.

Each filter is partial to at least one (sometimes two) primary (ies) of its own colour, and it absorbs some of the other primary (or primaries). Thus, a cyan filter favours blue and green and to some extent absorbs the third primary, red.

In general, filters are not used in black and white photography because their filtering action is not selective enough (their colour is too pale), and their effects remain practically unnoticed.

All filters require an increased exposure of $1/3$ to $1\frac{1}{3}$ stops, with the exception of the .05 yellow compensating filter which requires no exposure increase.

Filters are available with tinted glass and in sizes adaptable to the most common lenses. They are available, as well, in a square, coloured-gel format ranging in size upwards from 2 x 2 inches.

(Photo by R.W.) ➤

25 What is the function of a compensating filter?

Colour compensating filters, usually referred to as CC filters, come in the three primary colours: blue, green and red; and in the three secondary colours: yellow, magenta and cyan. For each of these six hues, there are six degrees of absorption, numbered according to their strength: .05, .10, .30, .40 and .50.

These filters are used in the enlarging of colour negatives, and they allow a good deal of control over the colour balance of the print.

They are also used in shooting. Despite the high degree of standardization maintained in the manufacture of photographic emulsions, it is impossible to assure absolute uniformity from one stock lot to the next. This means that one lot may give slides which have a certain dominant or false colour cast. For example, if the dominant is yellowish, you would use a blue CC filter to absorb it.

False coloration often passes unnoticed or may even be acceptable. On the other hand, when the high standards of professional work require absolute colour fidelity, the cast must be corrected with an appropriate filter.

At other times, one may want to introduce a false coloration deliberately in order to accentuate a particular characteristic of the subject in question: for example, a yellow or green .30 CC filter will lend added luminosity to a sunlight-dappled forest scene.

See colour plate 11

26

Slides taken with an indoor colour film (Ekta-chrome H.S. type B) under regular household lighting have a yellowish tint. What is the cause of this?

We know that there are two types of colour film for artificial light (apart from electronic flash). They are type A, which is balanced for photofloods, whose colour temperature is 3400°K, and type B (the more common) which is used with light of 3200°K. Now, the high sensitivity of certain emulsions (notably Ektachrome H.S. type B) permits snapshots in interiors lit only with domestic tungsten bulbs (60, 100, 150, 1000 W). But the colour temperature of these bulbs varies from about 2500 to 3000°K. This means that their spectral composition contains excessive yellow, by comparison with 3200-3400°K lamps. The weaker the bulb (25, 40, 60 W), the more pronounced the effect. The "hotter" tones obtained in this way are often very desirable. If, however, you want to eliminate this coloration, you would use a suitable bluish filter.

The same reasoning applies to untinted magnesium bulbs whose colour temperature is in the range of 4000°K, and which therefore have an excess of blue. A yellowish filter is required to eliminate the bluish dominant here.

This is the function of **light correction** filters. The 81 series, which are yellow in colour, lower the colour temperature of the light source, while the 82 series, which are blue, increase it (see table). To sum up, the 81 and 82 series filters adjust the colour temperature of light sources varying from 2500° to 4100°K, down to a range of 3200° to 3400°K.

Other uses may also be found for these filters. For example, a portrait lit only by blue sky shot on daylight colour film will have a bluish cast. A yellow 81A filter will produce better skin tones by removing some of the blue.

See colour plate 12

(Photo by R.W.) ▶

Light Correction Filters

Filters to raise the colour temperature (blue)				
82		to change 3,100°K to 3,200°K	or	3,290°K to 3,400°K
82A		to change 3,000°K to 3,200°K	or	3,180°K to 3,400°K
82B		to change 2,900°K to 3,200°K	or	3,060°K to 3,400°K
82C		to change 2,800°K to 3,200°K	or	2,950°K to 3,400°K
82C	+ 82	to change 2,720°K to 3,200°K	or	2,870°K to 3,400°K
82C	+ 82A	to change 2,650°K to 3,200°K	or	2,780°K to 3,400°K
82C	+ 82B	to change 2,570°K to 3,200°K	or	2,700°K to 3,400°K
82C	+ 82C	to change 2,490°K to 3,200°K	or	2,610°K to 3,400°K

Filters to reduce the colour temperature (yellow)			
81	to change 3,300°K to 3,200°K	or	3,510°K to 3,400°K
81A	to change 3,400°K to 3,200°K	or	3,630°K to 3,400°K
81B	to change 3,500°K to 3,200°K	or	3,750°K to 3,400°K
81C	to change 3,600°K to 3,200°K	or	3,850°K to 3,400°K
81D	to change 3,700°K to 3,200°K	or	3,970°K to 3,400°K
81EF	to change 3,850°K to 3,200°K	or	4,140°K to 3,400°K

27 I took some photos indoors with electronic flash. They came out blue although I was using an indoor colour film. What went wrong?

There are three types of colour slide film: the daylight type, and the tungsten light types A and B, also known as indoor film.

Each of them must be used with lighting that is of a specific colour temperature: 6000°K for daylight, 3400°K for type A (photoflood) and 3200°K for type B. When a film is used with a light source different from that which was meant for it, a false coloration or cast will result.

Electronic flash has a colour temperature of about 6000°K, which makes it **qualitatively** similar to daylight. A daylight-type emulsion is therefore required for indoor shooting with an electronic flash, rather than an indoor film, type A or B. Since electronic flash is richer in blues than tungsten lamps, this explains the blue colour cast on your slides.

It is nevertheless possible to use a film with a light source other than that for which it was balanced. Such a case arises sometimes when the camera is loaded with, for example, type B (3200°K) film, for tungsten light. After shooting indoors, you may still have several shots left that

you will not want to use with the same lighting. It is quite easy to finish off this roll either outdoors, or with electronic flash. The only precaution to be taken is to use the appropriate **conversion filter.**

Since daylight and electronic flash are richer in blue radiations than the light from tungsten lamps (3200°K) for which type B film is normally intended, the conversion filter's job will be to absorb this excess blue.

The table below indicates which filters to use in similar circumstances.

Slide

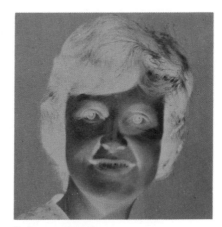

Colour negative

Colour photo

Black and white photo

Plate 1

1½ stops underexposure

Slight overexposure when duplicating (1 stop)

Plate 2

Infrared

Regular

Plate 3

Slide

Ektapan negative
(4 x 5 inches)

From the box below

Printed on Kodabromide No. 1

Plate 4

**Ektachrome X
— 1/60 sec. at f/11**

**High Speed Ektachrome, type B
— 1/250 sec. at f/8**

**Kodachrome II
— 1/60 sec.
at f/5.6**

Plate 5

**Ektachrome, type B ⅛ sec.
at f/11 — 2 100 W bulbs**

Plate 6

The original

The copy

Slide duplicator

Plate 7

High Speed Ektachrome 160 ASA shot at 300 ASA — 1/250 sec. at f/16 (special processing)

(Gaf)Anscochrome 500 ASA shot at 800 ASA — 1/1000 sec. at between f/16 and f/11 (special processing)

Plate 8

Type of film	Light source	Conversion filter
Daylight	3200 °K photo lamps	80A
(6000 °K)	2400 °K photoflood	80B
	Magnesium flash (Untinted)	80C or 80D
Type A (3400 °K)	Daylight or Electronic flash	85
Type B (3200 °K)	Daylight or Electronic flash	85B

(Photo by R.W.)

28 Should a correction filter always be used when the light source has a colour temperature different from that for which the film was balanced?

∎ ■ ∎ ■ ∎ ■ ∎ ■ ∎ ■ ∎ ■ ∎ ■ ∎ ■ ∎ ■ ∎ ■ ∎ ■ ∎ ■ ∎ ∎ ■ ∎

The preceeding questions have shown that using the wrong kind of light source will always result in a dominant coloration if no correction filter is used.

The table below gives a few examples of the false coloration you can expect when a colour film is not used according to the manufacturer's directions.

Type of film	Light source	Colour cast
Daylight	Blue sky only (subject in shade)	bluish
(6000 °K)	Overcast sky	bluish
	Daylight (sun and sky) in 2-hour period following the rising or preceding the setting of sun	yellow-orange
	Fluorescent bulbs	greenish (depending on type)
	All tungsten bulbs	yellow-orange (the lower the temperature the more orange the cast)
Type A (3400 °K)	Daylight (sun and sky)	blue
Type B (3200 °K)	Daylight (sky only)	blue
	Daylight (sunset)	more or less normal colour rendering
	Electronic flash	blue
	Blue magnesium flash	blue
	Untinted magnesium flash	bluish
	Fluorescent bulb	depends on type
	Domestic tungsten bulbs	yellow-orange

These dominants are almost always blue or yellow-orange, depending on whether the colour temperature of the light source is higher or lower than what it was supposed to be.

However, the serious photographer who wants to get past the stage of faithful and objective reproduction, and who wants to use photography as a means of personal expression, will soon see fit to break the rules to which he has adhered so closely up to that point.

He will then be able to experiment knowledgeably with emulsion/light source combinations which would normally be ill-advised. He might use light sources as different as electronic flash and tungsten lamps for the same shot. The photos in plate 13 provide a few examples of some of the possibilities.

See colour plate 13

(Photo by R.W.)

29 What are the differences between a photo printed from panchromatic film and one printed from orthochromatic film?

■ ■

Remember, first of all, that black and white photography involves a double transfiguration of reality: on the one hand, it converts three-dimensional space into a two-dimensional image, and on the other, it changes colours into grey tones. In order for this second change to be objectively satisfactory, the grey tones which are reproduced must give the same impression of luminosity as those colours of the photographed subject.

When you look at a lemon and a tomato, the luminosity of the yellow is greater than that of the red. This explains why the yellow appears pale grey and the red a darker grey in a black and white photograph.

For this to happen, the emulsion must have a colour sensitivity as similar as possible to that of the eye. It is this kind of film, called **panchromatic,** which both amateur and professional photographers use every day.

There are, on the other hand, certain circumstances which do not call for the same colour sensitivity. For example, in the printing industry where photo offset is used to reproduce black and white documents for printing in periodicals, **orthochromatic emulsions,** which are insensitive to red, are used.

Printers also make use of a third type of film called **nonchromatic** which is only sensitive to blue.

The visual effect of these sensitivity-selective emulsions varies. In the case of the orthochromatic emulsion, its non-sensitivity to red means that the red light reflected by objects of this colour will only darken the negative very slightly. During enlarging, this slight effect on the negative means considerable darkening of the positive print. Any red object or one containing a high proportion of red will appear as a very dark gray in a black and white photograph.

Similarly, the non-chromatic emulsion, whose **chromatic sensitivity** is limited to blue, renders the colours red, orange, yellow and green in greys that are much darker than normal. Although this is not acceptable when one is looking for an objective representation of reality, it must be remembered that creative expression often requires the controlled use of materials or pro-

cedures which are normally judg-
ed as erroneous.

See colour plate 14

(Photo by R.W.)

30 Which is better: the coupled rangefinder camera or the single lens reflex camera?

I have always been an ardent supporter of the coupled rangefinder camera, as opposed to the single-lens reflex, because I believe that despite certain advantages offered by the latter, the coupled rangefinder is superior in a good many other ways.

A Nikon-SP was my first camera: it served me well for 15 years and I still have it now. Many professionals share my opinion of the coupled rangefinder camera.

I consider the single-lens refe (SLR) camera absolutely indispensable in many cases, but when I have no particular idea for a photo in my head, or when it comes to most day-to-day-work, my preference is for the coupled range finder.

By way of comparison, here is a short list of the advantages and disadvantages of both:

(Photo by A.D.)

Coupled rangefinder (35mm)

Advantages

Very light

Silent

Small, compact

Mechanics reduced to a minimum — less possibility of breakdown

Very precise focussing, especially in weak lighting and for close-ups

Faster to handle when action accelerates.

Disadvantages

Some problems with parallax, especially close up

Impossible to ascertain the depth of field

The absence of any mirror allows shooting at very slow shutter speeds, for example 1/4 to 1/8 sec. even hand-held.

Single-lens reflex (35mm)

Advantages

Ideal for composing, especially for close-ups, macrophotography, etc.

No problem with parallax

Often equipped with a device for ascertaining the depth of field

Ideal and highly recommended for lenses l o n g e r than 135mm. Focussing advantage here.

Disadvantages

Rather heavy

Very noisy

A bit large

The movement of the mirror limits shooting at shutter speeds below 1/30 sec.

V e r y complicated mechanically; very expensive to have repaired.

The choice is yours!

31

Whenever I say I have an "Instamatic", people think I am talking about some cheap camera, yet it cost me more than $200. How would you explain this reaction?

Very few people know than an "Instamatic" camera is not necessarily cheap. Of course, the "instant loading" feature was first offered on fairly inexpensive cameras, but now this feature is offered on many other kinds of camera, some of which are very expensive.

It was only a few years ago that the manufacturers really began to look for ways to eliminate the time-consuming task of loading the camera. Automation had already simplified many other aspects of photography but loading the camera had always been an unresolved problem.

Now, after thirty-five years, a solution has been found!

Every amateur, or professional for that matter, has dreamed of the day when he could eliminate or speed up the awkward film loading process. Indeed, the professionals feel they ought to be the first to benefit from "magazine-loading" cameras.

Now they can. Hasselblad, Bronica and Contarex are among the manufacturers who have perfected interchangeable magazines which allow you to change from black and white to colour in the middle of a roll.

Most film cameras nowadays use cartridge-loaded film. This has eliminated the problem of threading for all but about 25% of amateur filmmakers. In my opinion, those manufacturers who have not done so already would do well to modify their camera body designs in order to accommodate cartridges. Everyone would benefit if they did.

A cartridge-loading camera like this sells for more than $200

instamatics start at about $25

32

I cannot understand why photos taken with my 35mm lens are more contrasty than those taken with my 135mm lens, even though they were developed in the same way. Is there something wrong with my telephoto?

There is nothing wrong with it at all.

You will always get a slightly "softer" photograph with a telephoto lens. The image being photographed with a telephoto lens must pass through fairly long stretches of atmospheric haze. In so doing, the image loses a certain amount of contrast. The result is inevitably a softer, greyer image.

Furthermore, the light transmission characteristics of one lens may differ somewhat from that of another, even at the same openings. In other words, an f/8 opening on a telephoto may give an image which is slightly underexposed by comparison with the f/8 on a 35mm lens. Such is the case with the Russian 500mm VTO catadioptric telephoto: the manufacturer claims it to be an f/8, whereas all the tests have shown that it is in fact an f/11. Hence, there is a noticeable underexposure every time you use it, unless the discrepancy is corrected.

To increase the contrast on an entire roll shot with a telephoto, it can be underexposed by one stop, then overdeveloped for three or four minutes with vigorous agitation. Alternatively, when shooting with a telephoto, use a contrast filter, either the green or red A filter, or Kodak's anti-ultraviolet 1A filter, which neutralizes atmospheric haze.

**135mm Nikkor lens — 1/250 sec.
at f/8, Plus-X 200 ASA
— D-76 9 min.**

33 Is 35mm, 2¼ x 2¼, or something larger, the ideal camera format?

■ ■

This question is not one that I like to answer, for I have little to say on the subject. In my opinion, the format is of little consequence in itself. It is really the content of the picture that is of greatest interest.

The 35mm camera has been popular for 20 years and shows no signs of falling out of favour. Some people feel that the 2¼ x 2¼ TLR (Twin Lens Reflex) has become an antique, and this is perhaps true for the amateur who does a lot of shooting. But the professional still makes use of it, and it is his camera of choice for certain kinds of commercial and industrial work. In some cases he will only to go 35mm if he has no other choice.

All press photographers use the 35mm format, for reasons too numerous to go into here. Because these cameras are small, the photographer can carry two or three with lenses of different focal lengths on each one. Moreover, they lend themselves to faster handling.

Each format has its advantages. Kodachrome II or X is only available in the 35mm format, which is a distinct advantage in itself. Many photographers, especially professionals, prefer 2¼ x 2¼

because it is a good compromise between 35mm and 4 x 5. It is not as hefty as the 4 x 5's, yet offers a high degree of definition. The format has its own advantages too; for example, parallel line correction and control of the depth of the field almost to infinity.

It is true, nonetheless, that the 4 x 5 and 8 x 10 formats allow a very high degree of technical polish. One has only to examine pages of the famous German magazines **Grossbild** and **International Photo Technik** to see the results (they use photos shot only with large-format cameras).

Note also that the smaller the camera, the more powerful the lenses the manufacturer can use.

I myself have long dreamed of owning a reflex camera in the "super slide" format, namely the **127 x 127**. For a long time now I have cut my 2¼ x 2¼ slides in order to obtin this format, which I find ideal. It allows me to use a 35mm projector and to fill the screen with practically twice the image.

There has been talk for years of putting a super-35mm camera on the market which, instead of giving an image of 24 x 36mm, would give a 28 x 42mm image by eliminating the perforations running along the side of the film. This is an excellent idea, but little progress seems to have been made in developing such a camera. There would be an increase of 35% in the image area over the original format.

Incidentally, architectural photography generally relies on the larger formats, 4 x 5 in. or 8 x 10 inches. However, custom did not prevent me from submitting a 16 x 20 in. photo to a very large architectural photography contest and capturing first prize for all of Canada. I shot that photo with a Nikon 35mm.

A $2500 pyramid. Take your choice: a 4 × 5 Graphic View, a 2¼ × 2¼ Hasselblad or a 35 mm Nikkormat

34 What special precautions should be taken when shooting in very cold weather?

■ ■

When the temperature is below 0°F, shutters have a particular tendency to stick, especially if the camera has not been cleaned recently.

A complete absence of image may result, or you may get overexposed images as a result of poor functioning of the light meter battery. This applies even to the famous CDS-PX625 mercury battery, which is supposed to offer better resistance to the cold than other batteries.

The traditional remedy for the problem of shooting in very cold weather is to keep the camera under your coat, as close as possible to your body, until the very moment you use it.

This will help to eliminate the problem of fog on the lens when you bring your camera from the cold into a warm room.

There is little point in loading a camera with **cold film.** It will undoubtedly break when you try to thread it. It may help if you blow on the threading tongue. The film rarely breaks once it has begun winding.

Professionals who have to work outdoors in very cold weather, (for example, reporters who must cover a sporting event which lasts two or three hours on a mid-January afternoon), will invest $50 to $75 in having their cameras treated against the cold. (This is a job which should be left to an expert.) You will then be able to shoot in weather of –50°F. There will be no need to keep the camera covered and it will perform without any problem.

With the temperature at —10 °F,
the camera should go right back
under your coat as soon as
the shot is taken, unless it
has been treated against cold.

35 If my film is scratched from one end to the other, do I blame the camera or the film?

■ ■

The film spools made by any reputable manufacturer are not likely to be the cause of the problem. We must therefore look elsewhere.

If you are among those who load their cassettes from bulk film, you might want to think of replacing your cassettes. Their lip constitutes a kind of dust trap. After they have been used a dozen times you should replace them, for the dust may scratch the film.

Chances are that your problems will be solved by giving the interior of the camera a good cleaning, especially those parts where the film comes in contact with metal. This should be done on a regular basis (see cleaning, Question 148).

Perhaps you simply wiped your film with a chamois or cloth that wasn't clean. A single small particle of dust is enough to scratch a film over its entire length.

Never clean a photo which has a large segment of sky, with a chamois or any other kind of cloth. You must be content to soak the film in a solution of "Photo-flo" and to let it dry as is.

You have probably seen dark lines in nicely photographed skies before. It always seems to happen to the best shots.

Fine black lines are usually caused by dust on the film. Retouching is a tricky process.

36 In your opinion, are the German cameras the best in the world?

■■■■■■■■■■■■■■■■■■■■■■■■■■■■■■■■■■■■

There is much truth in this statement.

The Germans have been world-leaders in precision manufacturing for generations. It has become an obsession with them and the products they manufacture are of the highest quality. The same goes for the Swiss with their watch-making and chronometer industries, and for the Swedes with their Hasselblad!

Among the many prestigious products manufactured in Germany we might mention Leica cameras; the subminiature Minox cameras; the Agfa 35mm coupled rangefinder cameras; the famous Linhof 2¼ x 3¼, 4 x 5 and 8 x 10; the Voigtlander and Zeiss cameras; the Leitz enlargers; and the Retina cameras manufactured in Germany by Kodak.

In laboratory trials Leica cameras were pushed to a half-million shots before they broke down. This means being able to shoot some 14,000 rolls of film of 36 frames before experiencing any difficulties!

It is interesting to note that the German manufacturers do not seem very worried by the stiff competition being offered by the Japanese. In fact a number of them seem to have slowed down production, preferring to manufacture one camera instead of ten in order to maintain performance standards which no other manufacturer can hope to meet. Leica now have trouble keeping up with demand, but their supremacy may not last forever. Keeping in mind the tenacity for with the Japanese are so famous, it is possible that their photographic products may be on their way to becoming world-beaters. Right now the Russions are starting out where the Japanese began ten years ago. Perhaps they will take over from the Japanese in their turn fifteen years from now. Moreover, there has been talk recently of a merger between Leica and Minolta.

A popular Japanese camera

**A German camera
with a good reputation**

37 I can't afford to buy a new camera. What advice do you have for someone buying a second-hand camera?

People should realize that if someone sells his camera or trades it in for a better one, it means, for the most part, that he is not satisfied with it. Will you be satisfied with it after you have bought it? Perhaps . . .

The idea of purchasing a second-hand camera from a store makes me uncomfortable. I do not wish to cast any doubt on the honesty of the majority of retailers, but after twenty-five years in the business I have met a few and they are all first-class SALES-MEN.

There are bargains around and there are always people interested in a bargain. But do not buy a camera just because it is a bargain. If at all possible, buy your camera from a friend, someone you know well. You will at least know something about him and above all how long he has had the camera. Because you know him well, you will also know how much wear-and-tear the camera has suffered.

Naturally you have always wanted a high-quality camera. You have convinced yourself that it is better to have a second-hand one than not at all. The only thing is, you have no way of knowing if your prestigious second-hand camera was owned by a professional who has simply worn it out. Cameras, unlike cars, have no mileage counters. You will realize eventually that this kind of economizing rarely makes sense.

You may get a one-month guarantee for your purchase, but beyond that you will have to repair it yourself, at great expense. If it happens to be an obsolete model, you will find that spare parts are no longer available. The salesman might "forget" to tell you that it isn't being made any more, and just try and sell it back to him!

If my views on the subject are rather pessimistic, it is because I know as a professional that it is not unusual to shoot 300 to 400 photos a day in the course of a long assignment. Add up the total for one year, or two or three. This is about the limit of a camera's life in the hands of a professional.

A camera is very delicate piece of machinery. In general, its outward appearance will tell you a good deal about how it has been treated. Even so, you should not put all your trust in appearances. Although some people rarely use their cameras, they may have no idea whatsoever about how to take care of them. (See Question 148)

When you make your purchase, ask the salesman to let you try out the camera for a few days, even if it means leaving a deposit (watch his reaction). Take this opportunity to have the camera checked over by a competent technician. Only he can advise you about the wisdom of your purchase.

The second-hand camera dealers in whom I have confidence are not very numerous. You may be fortunate in finding a good second hand dealer. If so, by all means buy from him — but have the camera checked by a technician first. In any case, be careful.

A big sale . . .

Please leave repairs to the experts!

38 Why do manufacturers make their cameras in two different finishes, one black and the other chrome? Which would you recommend?

The reason is very simple: the manufacturers are catering to the wishes of certain photographers who, because of the nature of their work, want to be as inconspicuous as possible. A camera with a shiny chrome finish is more conspicuous than one which is matte black.

Thus, most press photographers work with black-finish cameras.

Some photographers believe that it is better to use a black camera in cold weather and a shiny camera in hot weather. They base their reasoning on the principle of absorption and reflection of light — and of heat. I am rather doubtful about this. Until I hear more convincing reasons, I will continue to believe that this is merely a question of taste.

Note that a black-finish body costs about 10% to 15% more than an aluminum-finish body.

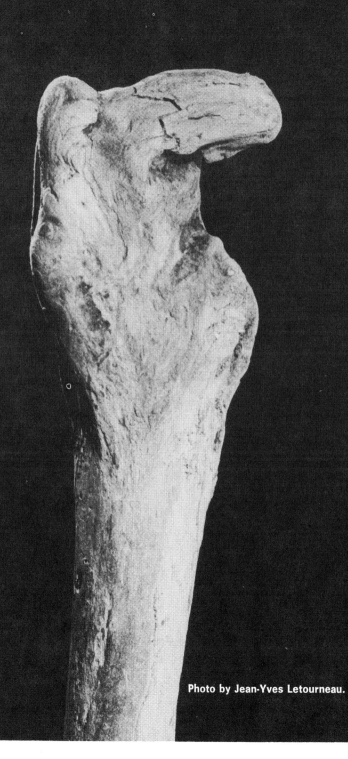

39
How do you account for such a wide price range in 35mm SLR cameras, even though they all work the same way? What kind do you use?

■ ■

You can purchase a 35mm (reflex) camera for as little as $35. The same retailer can also sell you a nice-looking model for as much as $900.

I think you will begin to find an answer to this question by examining the qualities of precision, durability and longevity that the merchandise offers. Despite the diversity of their prices, the SLR's all seem to have the same characteristics. The mind boggles at what certain manufacturers must have to do to produce some cameras at such low prices.

When I am on assignment for *La Presse,* I use the equipment which is given to me, that is, 2 Nikons with 3 lenses: 21mm, 85mm and 135mm. My own equipment includes a Pentax Spotmatic, a Leica M3, a Hasselblad and a Graphic View 4 x 5.

(Photo by A.D.) ➤

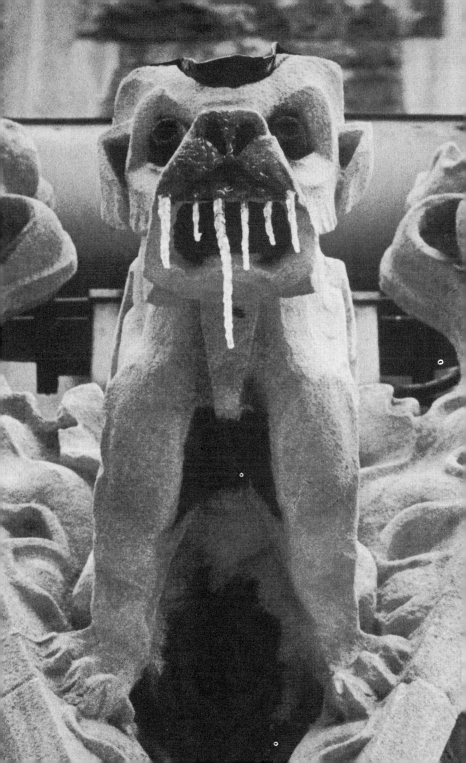

40 Is it possible to buy a "good quality" reflex camera for less than $75?

Definitely! There is a Russian camera called the Zenit-B, which is available from some camera merchants.

It is a mystery to me how it is possible to make an inexpensive reflex featuring interchangeable lenses, opening to f/2.8, with shutter from 1/500 to 1/30 sec., and X-synchronization for flash — but the Russians have done so — and moreover, the price is less than $50.00. Presumably, a Russian manufacturer is willing to cut costs in order to break into the American market and capture some of the territory held by the Japanese.

The Zenit-B does, however, have fewer features than the more expensive SLR's. This includes the absence of automatic aperture control, non-return of the mirror after each exposure, no simplified frame-counter, lack of built-in light meter, no shutter speed lower than 1/30 sec. and slow re-winding mechanism.

For the beginner on a tight budget, however, this camera has much to offer. It has a delayed shutter release, it is fairly quiet, and the winding knob is reasonably solid. Visibility through the pentaprism is excellent, as good as with more costly cameras. As a matter of fact, its optical system compares favourably with that of any camera which sells for five times the price. (See Question 49)

As for its longevity, it is too soon to make any judgment, but I am confident that it will not disappoint the "Sunday photographer".

Unfortunately, it is not possible to buy this camera everywhere. One salesman told me recently that merchants did not wish to sell it because its low price did not permit a high enough profit!

Very recently there has been word of a new model — the Zenit-E — which has just appeared on the market, and which is greatly improved. Its price is reported to be in the region of $65.

CAMERA
REFLEX

ZENIT

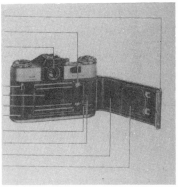

latch of the lock
sprocket
viewfinder eyepiece

cassette spool guide
film gate
film channel slides
cassette chamber
take-up spool
take-up spool spring
camera back cover
film pressure table

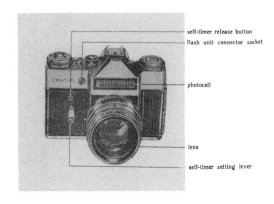

self-timer release button
flash unit connector socket

photocell

lens

self-timer setting lever

41 Now that we have multicoated lenses, is there any need to have a sunshade or lens-hood on the lens?

■ ■

Multicoating is a real blessing. However, it cannot replace a lens-hood. The purpose of multi-coating is to cut down on stray reflections in the lens and to improve the quality of the contrast.

Undesirable reflections cannot always be blamed on the lens itself. More often than not, they are simply the result of shooting without a lens-hood.

Watch a professional at work; you might be surprised to see him using not only a lens-hood but also a kind of sunshade which resembles the old bellows device. He will not be using it for its decorative value. On the contrary, he is very aware of stray light which can fog up the film or create hexagonal blotches of light.

The advantage of this kind of sunshade is that it can be adjusted to suit all focal lengths. It will mask all light superfluous to the exposure. The clarity and definition of the images it produces must be seen to be appreciated.

You should never do any shooting without a sunshade. I think that it is the most indispensable of all accessories.

Sunshades made of rubber will also help protect the lens from damage.

You are always further ahead using a sunshade — the best possible.

Helios 58mm lens (on a Zenith). The main problem with these cheaper lenses is their inability to overcome backlighting problems (like this) even with a sunshade.

Takumar multicoated lens (on a Pentax), plus sunshade.

42 Is the difference between type A and type B colour film so critical that you really cannot use a photoflood (3400° K) with type B?

■ ■

Photofloods are balanced for type A emulsions. This means that their light tends more toward blue than ordinary boosted lamps for type B (3200°K).

If you use photofloods, therefore, you risk getting a false rendering of skin tones which will come out too "cool" or even blue. (See Questions 2, 26, 27 and 75)

We know that there are two different series of correction filters available — the 82's, which are bluish and serve to raise the colour temperature of a light source, and the 81's, which are "hot" or yellowish and serve to lower the colour temperature.

Fortunately, these correction filters do not affect the chromatic balance of your film when they alter the colour temperature.

For the case in question, since a type B emulsion is being used (much more popular than the type A emulsions), what is needed is an 81A correction filter, which heats up the overly blue (3400°K) light by lowering it to 3200°K.

Note that you will have to increase the diphragm opening by ⅓ stop; this will compensate for the loss of light caused by the filter.

Many filmmakers who work in colour — especially for television — use an emulsion balanced for artificial light (type A or B) almost exclusively. When they have to film outdoors, they simply apply an 85 or 85B conversion filter, and after a slight adjustment in the ASA rating they can continue shooting without any problem. It is much easier to keep a couple of filters in your pocket than to change film every time you move outside from inside, or vice versa. Apart from giving excellent results, this system makes for savings in footage, and more efficient editing.

See question 41, bottom of the page. Tri-X 1/500 sec. at f/8.

43 Should an anti-ultraviolet filter always be left on the camera to protect the lens?

■ ■

Certain kinds of low power lens, like the f/4.5's and f/5.6's let in a good deal of ultraviolet radiation, because of the reduced number of elements involved (usually two or three). If a camera lacks an anti-reflective or other correcting device, a 1-A filter should be left on at all times.

It is unnecessary to leave one of these filters on a modern f/1.4 or f/2.8 lens, since they have usually been treated for every conceivable problem.

The 1-A filter, which is practically colourless, offers efficient protection against water, snow and sand, as well as against the fingerprints of curious children. Using this filter on a fast modern lens, however, would be a little like putting triple storm windows on your house.

If your camera is rather old, it is a good idea to leave this filter on the lens, especially if you are in the habit of carrying it around without a case.

The antiultraviolet Skylight 1-A filter

Plus-X, 1/250 sec. at f/8

Plus-X, 1/60 sec. at f/16

44 How can I eliminate the blue cast I always get in my snow shots?

∎∎∎∎∎∎∎∎∎∎∎∎∎∎∎∎∎∎∎∎∎∎∎∎∎∎∎∎∎

Use a coloured filter — namely, the Kodak Wratten 1-A Skylight Filter. It will absorb the ultra-violet, blue-violet and even some of the green radiations. The pale pink tint is too weak to affect the other colours in your shots.

While this blue dominant is practically imperceptible to the naked eye when shooting, it is invariably captured on the photographic emulsion. It is particularly noticeable on bright surfaces (snow, water, sand), in shadows, in mountain scenes and when the landscape being photographed stretches to infinity. The use of a telephoto lens greatly amplifies the diffusion of ultraviolet radiation.

A photograph or slide with a blue dominant is considered "cold". The use of an ultraviolet filter (1-A, 2-A or 3-A, depending on the degree of correction desired) will help to warm up all the other colours in the picture.

This blue cast is naturally more marked whenever the sky is clear and blue; it tends to disappear as the sky becomes overcast or the weather foggy.

See colour plate 15

(Photo by A.D.)

45 Is it true that certain lenses give better definition (more precision) at about f/8 or f/5.6 than at f/22?

This is not a matter of mere opinion but of rigorous optical fact. Yet, I do not want to overemphasize its importance.

To understand the reasons for better definition at f/8 or f/5.6 requires a detailed study of the phenomenon of light diffraction, which is closely connected to that of the circles of diffusion.

Diffraction occurs at the periphery of the diaphragm and tends to create a rather diffuse image on the film. This diffusion is less noticeable with wider openings.

The circles of diffusion are points of light refracted by a lens element onto the focal plane, where they form an image of the object being photographed. These circles become smaller as the diaphragm becomes smaller.

It is therefore true that the resolving power of a lens is at its maximum about three stops down from its maximum aperture, or four for an f/1.4 lens.

Stopping down will increase the depth of field, but may have an adverse effect on the clarity of the image in terms of resolving power.

105mm lens — 1/1000 sec. at f/4 with two 4X neutral density filters. The box is in focus, but the depth of field is nil.

Same lens, same distance but stopped down to f/22. The box is still in focus and the depth of field is greatly improved.

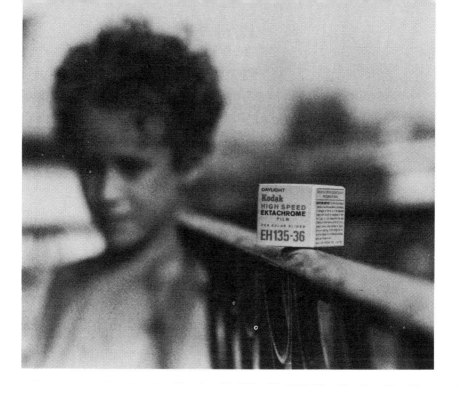

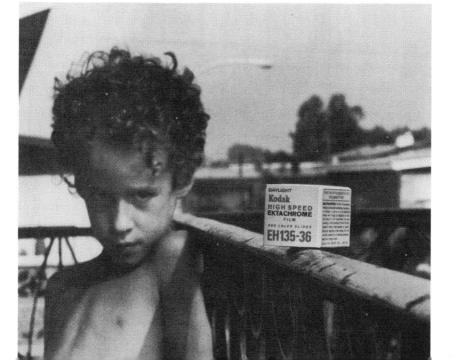

46 I have noticed that the image I get in my viewfinder (reflex) does not correspond exactly to the one I get in the picture. It is in fact slightly smaller. Is this normal?

■ ■

It is normal — and desirable too. Almost every enlarger made is designed to **mask** just a little of the film image all around the edge, and thereby prevent stray light from affecting the contrast of the picture.

The same explanation applies to slide mountings which take up to 1/16 in. from the edge of the picture.

Seeing a little less of the image on film than in reality gives you a certain safety margin.

For example, if you want to copy photos and get them full frame, you will have to move in a little closer to your subject. Note that negatives are rarely printed full frame. They are almost always cropped a little here or there in order to make up for errors of composition. The 35mm format does not correspond at all with the standard 8 x 10 in. enlarging format.

(Photo by A.D.)➤

47 Do zoom lenses give as sharp an image as lenses of fixed focal length?

In general, a standard fixed focal length 50mm lens worth $100 will be inferior in quality to a 43-86mm zoom lens costing $250.

It is always said that quality increases in proportion with cost. Popular belief also asserts that, for a given focal length, the definition offered by a zoom lens is not as good as that offered by an ordinary lens of good quality. Personally, I can seldom find any difference between two photos of the same format (8x10 in.) shot with a zoom lens and a fixed lens respectively.

All the critics agree that the precision of a zoom lens varies to some extent with the focal length: in fact, it is very precise at its greatest focal length and less so at its shortest.

I have no preference for one brand or another. If I use a zoom it is for reasons of speed and efficiency, but I am also aware that these advantages entail a certain sacrifice in quality.

Here is the range of focal lengths covered by the Nikkor zoom lens (f/3.5, 43-86mm):

a) 43mm

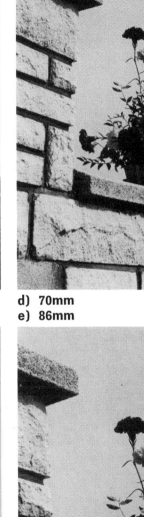

b) 50mm
c) 60mm

d) 70mm
e) 86mm

48 How useful are doublers or triplers?

Of all the photographic gadgets on the market today, these are among the most interesting.

These little lenses have been designed specifically to turn a normal lens into a telephoto.

By placing a doubler or tripler between the camera and the main lens, the focal length is automatically doubled or tripled. If you have a 50mm, the doubler will transform it into a 100mm. If you have a 100mm, the doubler will make it a 200mm.

If you instal a tripler, your 50mm lens will become a 150mm lens. If your lens is 200mm, the tripler will transform it into a 600mm. This is when it starts to get interesting!

If you consider that the price of a good 200mm lens is about $200, whereas you can achieve the same results by spending $25 or $30 on a doubler (converter), you will see that it is worth the investment.

The accessory needs of this lens — filters, hood, etc. — remain just the same.

As for quality, it is very acceptable.

Moreover, if you vary the shutter speed instead of the aperture, **you get the same depth of field** with this new telephoto as with the normal lens.

Another advantage: the lens/doubler combination is much lighter and easier to handle than the equivalent telephoto.

Doublers and triplers can also be adapted to zoom lenses with good results.

The only problem is a loss of luminosity in the order of two stops with the doubler and three stops with the tripler. The light meter will pick this up automatically.

Sometimes you will find that a lens will produce a "hot spot" in the centre of the image. This is considered a defect and reputable merchants will normally be pleased to exchange such a lens as long as you bring in proof in the form of a few spoiled photos.

Photo shot with normal lens: Tri-X — 1/500 at f/16

Same lens with a doubler
(2X). The 55mm lens
becomes a 110mm —
Tri-X — 1/500 at f/8.

Same lens with a tripler (3X).
The 55mm lens becomes a 150mm Tri-X — 1/500 at f/5.6.

49 Is one brand of lens really superior to another? What do you think of the less expensive lenses made by such firms as Soligor, Vivitar and Spiratone?

It is my opinion that a $450 Leica lens, a $1200 Hasselblad lens, or a $500 Nikon lens is of higher quality than a lens of the same power and focal length which sells for $50.

The lens elements used by Soligor, Vivitar and Spiratone are all made in Japan, and all originate in the same factories. This is not surprising since 80% of the photographic materials in the world come from this country. This also explains the very low cost of much of the equipment produced in Japanese plants.

I do not think that the differences in price and quality are only a factor of the optics; it is greatly a factor of the mechanics of the lenses. Cheap materials are used in the production of cheap lenses. Diaphragms operate according to different principles in the cheaper lenses than in those which are more expensive. The springs, the screws and the metals are all of inferior quality.

Moreover, the manufacturers of economy lenses will probably be the first to perfect plastic lenses in an attempt to corner the world market. Keep in mind that the vast majority of amateurs (more than 95%) never exceed the 8 x 10 in. format when it comes to printing. In sizes below this format, lens quality does not really show through in the finished product.

A good lens will rarely give you problems with the focussing or aperture rings.

As far as I am concerned, there is no reason not to purchase a 200mm lens for $150, provided that I cannot afford to pay $400. Since I would be concerned about mechanical defects, I would therefore handle a cheaper lens with the greatest care. I do know that some of these cheaper lenses are of reasonable quality; the only question is, how long will they last?

50 With a special adaptor, is it possible to invert the lens on a camera to do macrophotography?

This device is one of many accessories available to the photographer nowadays.

Most modern lenses are made in such a way that a filter or lenshood (or both) can be **screwed** onto a front mounting. The manufacturers have also created a simple adaptor ring which can be screwed on in place of a filter.

The opposite side of the ring is either threaded or has a bayonet mount. When you remove the lens from the body, you have only to turn it around and, depending on the type of camera, screw it or pop it into place again.

You will then notice an increase in the image size by about 1½ to 2 times.

You will also notice that the focussing has become practically fixed at about 4 inches. There is no point in turning the focussing has become practically fixed at about 4 inches. There is no point in turning the focussing ring back and forth, because the change is practically nil.

This produces an image which tends to be very focussed in the centre and very fuzzy towards the edges. Compare this to the explosive effect of a zoom lens. . . .

Remember that when you reverse the lens in this way the light meter mechanism will be disconnected. You should therefore take a reading before inverting the lens.

It is best to set up on a tripod and move the object to be photographed backwards or forwards in relation to the camera.

This ring allows you to put the lens on the camera backwards.

**With the lens on backwards
in this manner, you can shoot
up to 4 in. (10 cm).**

51 What is the difference between a lens which is "preset" and one which is not?

A preset lens is not designed to **close down automatically** to a desired aperture when the shot is taken.

Reflex cameras allow you to aim, focus and take a meter reading while the diaphragm is wide open.

With an automatic lens, you stop down, depending on the meter reading, to, say, f/11 or f/16, but the diaphragm will remain wide open even after you have stopped down on the aperture ring in order to let in the maximum amount of light for framing and focussing.

An automatic lens has a device which closes the diaphragm to the predetermined aperture in a fraction of a second, just as the shutter mechanism is activated. It happens so quickly that the photographer will not be aware of any loss of light.

With a preset (non-automatic) lens, however, the diaphragm must be **re-opened manually** every time you want to focus or take a reading. This lens is equipped with a special ring for presetting a desired aperture. It allows you to stop the aperture ring at the correct setting, but you still have to close the diaphragm **manually** just before the shot and while you are still looking through the viewfinder. This causes a considerable loss of light as the picture is taken.

Obviously, the preset type of lens is much cheaper than the automatic type. The beginner will soon realize, however, that it is very annoying to stop down at the very moment when he is trying to concentrate most on his subject. This makes it easy to forget the last minute adjustment of the diaphragm; the photo, of course, will then be over-exposed.

The preset lens

The arrow indicates the little device that activates the diaphragm of an automatic lens.

The preset diaphragm indicates f/11 on the chrome ring.
The lower ring indicates f/3.5 (this is the aperture ring).

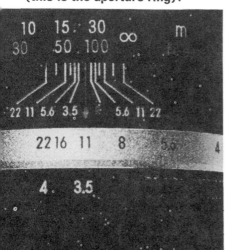

You close the black diaphragm ring just before shooting: it will stop automatically at the right spot.

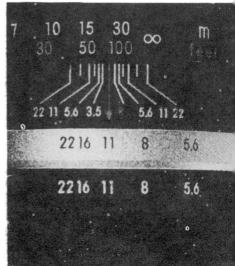

52

Why can one 52mm f/1.8 lens cost almost twice as much as another lens of the same focal length and power made by a different manufacturer?

The difference in price is determined primarily by the way the lenses are manufactured and the kind of glass used.

Glass is made from rare substances like thorium and zirconium, which are treated or cooked at temperatures of up to 800°F. for days or even weeks.

The manufacturing process is long, complicated and tedious. The most critical standards must be maintained in order to produce lens elements with precisely calculated curvatures, indices of refraction, etc.

That is why the quality controls on the production of some lenses are more exacting. You will recall that cheaper lenses lack proper anti-reflection protection. (See Question 41)

The illustration on the opposite page demonstrates that most manufacturers of lenses do maintain a certain standard of quality. Try to discern the difference between the two photos. One was shot with a Nikkor 52mm f/1.4 lens which costs about $250. The other was shot with a Zenith 58mm lens which is worth only $35 or $40. In the case of close ups printed on paper no larger than 8x10 in., it is difficult to tell at first glance which photo was shot with which lens. Does the quality difference justify the great difference in price? Look carefully before deciding on your answer.

In the final analysis, of course, you always get what you pay for. But all the same, it is a little too easy to exaggerate the importance of quality, sharpness, definition and resolving power when discussing lenses.

These 2 shots were done in the same way:
ASA 400 — 1/500 at f/8 — D-76 printed on Brovira No. 3

Which is which?

The photo on the left was taken with a Nikkor f/1.4

53 Do you think that a directional light meter or spot meter is a luxury for an amateur?

No light meter — spot meter or otherwise — is a luxury. It is a necessary piece of equipment. The proof of this lies in the fact that virtually every good reflex camera has a built-in light meter. Nevertheless, it is mainly professionals, or at least advanced amateurs, who use spot meters. This is because the device must be handled with the greatest care. Spot meters can be compared to directional microphones, which are aimed at someone who is talking at a distance of, say, 50 or 100 feet; they can isolate and capture this person's voice while at the same time eliminating unwanted background noise.

There is a greater tendency to make built-in light meters more and more directional. On some models, the reading angle has been reduced by as much as 50% to 75%. This produces a very concentrated reading.

Like the directional microphone, the basic characteristic of the spot meter is that it isolates one part of the subject and analyzes its brightness, independent of the rest of the scene. You know how difficult it is to shoot a back-lit subject with a light meter that reads the whole scene. In such a case you have to take readings from different parts of the scene one by one in order to avoid underexposing the main subject, especially when shooting a close-up portrait. At the request of professional photographers, the manufacturers have perfected light meters with a very reduced field. Some meters which require very delicate handling have a field of only four or five degrees.

A spot meter is necessary when the photographer is working at a distance from his subject. Take, for example, the problem of shooting a theatre scene from 50 or 100 feet. It would be impossible to do this with an ordinary light meter, whether built-in or separate from the camera. Theatre lighting relies heavily on "spots", which leave perhaps 90% of the stage in complete darkness. Hence, there is a necessity for a light meter with a reduced field.

If you are a real perfectionist (as all of us should be), and you shoot a lot of colour, then a spot meter would be a good investment. However, do not buy one which is centre-weighted. You will be best off with one that analyzes the subject mainly within a circle of 8 to 15 degrees. A selective reading of certain parts of the image allows a better exposure for those parts, but only at the expense of other areas of the picture. Read the instructions which come with your spot meter carefully. Remember that your need for a spot meter — or any other kind of specialized equipment — is always a function of the degree of technical excellence you expect from your photographs.

With the light meter pointed at the sky, there will be a strong reading and the main subject will be underexposed.

**This is a good way to get nice silhouettes . . .
ASA 400 — 1/1000 sec. at f/16.**

With the reading divided between the lightest and darkest areas, the picture is much more life-like. ASA 400 — 1/500 sec. at f/16.

Finally, with the meter pointed right into the shadowy area, the reading is very weak and all the detail in the shadowy area is brought out. ASA 400 1/250 sec. at f/11.

54 How can I most effectively use the famous Kodak "Neutral Density Test Card"?

The photos on the opposite page show you where the card should be used.

Here is a situation in which it is almost impossible to take a direct reading by reflected light since 99% of the surface to be photographed is either black or white.

A reading by incident light would be more appropriate. There is no point in trying to get a reading from the coin; in order to do so, you are likely to create a shadow which will spoil the reading.

The simplest, safest solution is to use the Kodak Neutral Density Test Card. The card has a grey side which reflects 18% of the light and a white side which reflects 90% (available at a photographic supply shop for about $1.50).

By placing the grey side in front of the camera, you can get a standard reflected light reading which will give good results. Just to make sure, take two photos, each ½ stop on either side of the indicated exposure.

When the lighting is very weak, it is better to use the white side of the card. For example, when the meter needle will not move any more, put the card, white side up, in front of the subject and add three stops to the new reading; or, use this reading, but be sure to divide the ASA of your film by five.

The grey card, then, gives an average reading at a glance, and dispenses with the need to average a series of readings.

Taking a reflected light reading on the Kodak Neutral Density Test Card. Ideal when there is a wide range of light values in the subject.

Here is a typical situation in which it is difficult to get a reading with a reflected-light exposure meter. This calls for either a neutral density card or an incident-light exposure meter.

55

When I photograph a subject with strong back-lighting, why does the subject always come out too dark? Is there something wrong with my light meter?

∎∎∎∎∎∎∎∎∎∎∎∎∎∎∎∎∎∎∎∎∎∎∎∎∎∎∎∎∎∎

The problem is not with your light meter.

Without being aware of it, you have been taking readings designed for silhouette shots. Since your light meter cannot think for itself, it has simply analyzed the entire image. The presence of bright blacklighting has caused the meter to give a "strong" reading and a "short" exposure time, hence the underexposure of the main subject.

As a first precaution, you should move closer to your subject and take a reading of it alone, thereby avoiding interference from the backlight.

A word of advice: learn to take advantage of your errors; you can learn to shoot interesting silhouette effects while experimenting with backlit shots.

Here is a typical situation in which it is difficult to get a reading with a reflected-light exposure meter. This calls for either a neutral density card or an incident-light exposure meter.

The built-in meter reading is much too strong (backlight). ASA 400 — 1/500 sec. at f/16.

Reading taken on the
photographer's hand
in the same plane
as the subjects.
ASA 400 — 1/500 sec.
at f/8.

56 How do I know when the mercury battery in my light meter is about to go dead?

■ ■

These batteries usually last for two years. Check the specifications as listed by the manufacturer.

Some meters do not have an off switch, which means that the battery will run down more quickly.

Mercury batteries can be counted on to give an even flow of power, but they die very abruptly, often in the space of an hour or less.

Obviously, you should not aim the meter at an intense light source for long periods of time.

After a year's use, check your battery periodically, either by comparing your meter's readings with those of a friend's, or else by closely inspecting the density of your films especially under normal lighting conditions.

It is a good habit to replace a battery at the same time every year.

It is a good idea to check the mercury battery from time to time to make sure the contacts are clean.

57

Which of the following works best: a) a separate light meter for incident light; b) a separate light meter for reflected light; or c) a built-in meter, that is, one that comes with the camera?

■ ■

The best way to get an accurate reading is to take it at the most critical point, that is, where the light strikes the surface of the emulsion.

You cannot expect a photo-electric cell to give an accurate analysis of how a subject is lit if the light meter in question is for incident light. It cannot take peculiarities of the subject into account, especially in close-ups. The reflected-light exposure meter does a better job in this respect, but because it is a separate accessory, it makes for awkward handling. In any case, it is more important to analyze the light reflected by a subject than that which falls on the subject.

The built-in light meter, coupled to the diaphragm represents, in my opinion, the most important discovery of the decade. The light is registered at the same point as it imprints the film. The meter will account for any filter which is being used on the camera. Apart from rapidity, it allows you to keep your eye on the view-finder and to concentrate on the framing.

The built-in light meter, in my estimation, represents as much of a step forward as the introduction of the reflex camera represented an advance over coupled-rangefinder cameras.

A manual light meter.
The bulb at the left "reads"
the reflected light

When moved to the centre,
it "reads" the incident light.

A through-the-lens metering
system. A photo-electric cell
located near the focal plane
or on the mirror analyzes
the light coming in.

A built-in meter system,
which requires adjustments
by hand.

58

I understand that SLR cameras (with built-in meter) automatically compensate for any filter which is on the lens. Is this true in all cases?

This is not true in all cases. However, with any weakly tinted filter, such as those in pale yellow, green, orange or neutral, you can assume that your reading is absolutely correct.

The meter reading may not be accurate with very dark filters, like dark green or dark red, since some dominant colours can affect the chromatic sensitivity of the cell. In these cases, you should keep in mind the coefficient indicated for the filter in question, and make an approximate "manual" comparison between readings **with** and **without** the filter.

As for ND-2X and 4X (neutral density) filters, the meter will make precise allowances for them, as the photos opposite indicate.

The meter "reads" the light reflected by the subject and the needle moves to 19.

When the photo-electric cell is covered with an NX-4X neutral density filter, the needle only moves to 17, which means the exposure must be increased by 2 stops.

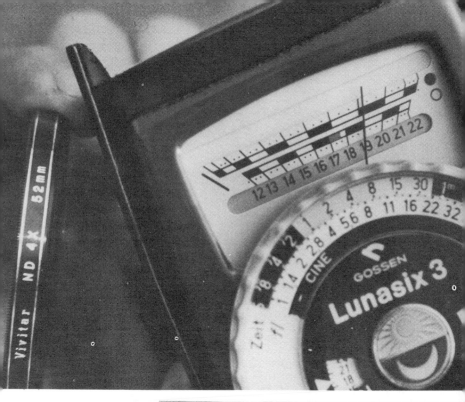

59 Does using bounced light from a flash always mean a change in aperture of two stops?

∎∎∎∎∎∎∎∎∎∎∎∎∎∎∎∎∎∎∎∎∎∎∎∎∎∎∎∎∎∎

There is some truth to this general rule, but only under the following conditions:

a) the subject being photographed must be in an average-size room, i.e., about 8 feet by 12 feet;

b) the ceiling must be **white** and the walls fairly **pale.**

Direct flash from 10 ft. (3m), at f/11.

Flash bounced off the ceiling and the rear wall, at f/5.6. Note the absence of shadow.

60

The flash on my Instamatic functions only about 50% of the time. Is there a sure-fire solution to this annoying problem?

■■■■■■■■■■■■■■■■■■■■■■■■■■■

First, determine the cause of the problem. If your Instamatic is one of the first models with a pop-up reflector dish, there may be a loose connection or the batteries may be weak or dead. It is also possible that there are impurities on the contact points of the batteries. Kodak is now producing a new Instamatic X series which uses the "Magicube" flash bulb. The first Instamatic models are no longer being made.

First designed by the Sylvania Company, the Magicube is a revolutionary new bulb which goes off without any battery. Of the one billion, six hundred million flash bulbs used every year in North America, at least 150 million do not function. The Magicube has put an end to most of these problems.

Magicubes function like the firing mechanism in a gun. Each lamp (there are four to a cube) has a small explosive tube which goes off under the impact of a spring. The spring is released when the camera shutter is pressed. Naturally, this mechanism is synchronized with the diaphragm and the shutter speed. After every shot, the Magicube automatically advances a quarter turn, so that the flash is positioned for the next shot. An indicator in the viewfinder lets you know if the flash functioned or not. We are told that it functions successfully 99.9% of the time.

It is safe to say that the era of the battery flash is dead. Sooner or later all magnesium flash will be equipped with this device, or one like it.

61 What is meant by the letters X, F, M or FP that are found on the lenses or bodies of cameras?

There are two kinds of shutter in common use — the **diaphragm** shutter and the **focal plane** shutter. The letters correspond to a certain type of flash synchronization which is used with one or the other.

The letter X applies to the focal plane shutter and is for all types of electronic flash used at shutter speeds of 1 second to 1/60 second. The letter F applies to the focal plane shutter and is for PF or AG magnesium bulbs (untinted or blue) at 1 second to 1/60 second. The letter M is for PF or AF magnesium bulbs, at speeds recommended by the manufacturer, usually covering the whole range offered by the diaphragm shutter.

The letters FP are for long-burning bulbs, that is, bulbs which burn long enough to permit the shutter to cross the film (FP — focal plane).

Even with a diaphragm shutter (see opposite), it is important to connect your electronic flash by the letter X and your magnesium flash by the letter M — since the timing of the electrical contact varies from one type of bulb to another.

For the focal plane shutter,
1 sec. to 1/60 sec.

M indicates synchronization
for all magnesium lamps
(SC or AG).

62 I received a camera and an electronic flash as gifts. However, there is no indication given as to the guide number or the shutter speed which will assure the best synchronization. When I tried to take a number of shots outside in the sun (with the flash) I got a double ghost image. How can I correct this problem?

∎ ∎

Never shoot a moving subject with electronic or magnesium flash outdoors (whether it is sunny or not). Electronic flash can only be synchronized with slow shutter speeds (1/30 to 1/60, sometimes 1/125 sec.) or, specifically, with focal plane shutters. The daylight hits the film before, during and after the flash does, thus causing the ghost, double image or blur.

Indoors, it is very easy to determine the guide number which corresponds to the intensity of the flash. To do so, you should be shooting in a medium-sized room, 10 ft. by 12 ft., with the subject approximately ten feet away. Shoot a series of exposures at f/4, f/5.6, f/8 and f/11. After developing and printing each shot, you will be able to see clearly which one best resembles a normal exposure. For example, if the photo shot at f/8 seems the best and your subject was ten feet away, your guide number for this particular flash will be 80 (f/8 x 10) from now

on. In another situation, you might shoot something from four feet away. You must then divide your guide number (80) by 4, which equals 20. Your aperture will therefore be f/22, the one closest to the figure 20.

Note that the guide number corresponds to the particular sensitivity rating of the film being used. For 160 ASA, the guide number is 80. If you use a slower emulsion some other time, say 80 ASA (half of 160 ASA), you must divide the guide number by 1.4 (the square root of 2), to get a new number, 57. Similarly, if your film is 320 ASA (twice 160 ASA), the guide number would change from 80 to 160. You would then have to do the test shots described above.

It is very useful to make a note of the three most important combinations right on the camera:

160 ASA, guide number 80 =

10 ft. at f/8, 7 ft. at f/11 and 5 ft. at f/16.

In order to determine the shutter speed which synchronizes best with your flash (with a focal plane shutter), simply take a few shots at the following speeds: 1/250, 1/125, 1/60 and 1/30. Then choose the speed which gives you the best image, free of any black line caused by the shutter's partial obstruction of the image. The manufacturer usually recommends s h u t t e r speeds lower than 1/125 sec. except, of course, in the case of diaphragm shutters. These can be synchronized up to 1/500 second. The best way to get to know your equipment is to make errors deliberately.

This blur was caused by shooting at too low a shutter speed (1/60 sec.), with fast flash, on a moving subject.

Only a diaphragm shutter (at 1/500 sec.) can overcome this problem.

63 How do I use a "flash exposure meter"?

A flash exposure meter is an extremely useful tool generally used in large commercial studios. It is about the same size as an ordinary light meter and costs between $80 and $150. The photographer holds it in front of the most important part of his subject, with the flash meter facing the camera, and then fires his electronic flash. The light it produces activates the photo-electric cell in the meter. It, in turn, activates the galvanometer needle, which will register f/16 or f/8 or f/11. The indicated aperture will be perfectly accurate. The sensitivity rating of the film must, of course, be set on the meter beforehand. The shutter speed becomes much less critical in conjunction with electronic flash. Its "flash" is rarely slower than 1/1000 sec.; it is usually of the order of 1/2000 to 1/10,000 sec. This means that even at a shutter speed of 1/500 sec. (which is very slow by comparison with 1/10,000), all of the light produced by the flash will be easily picked up in the time the shutter remains open. This statement of course refers to a diaphragm shutter.

The flash meter is especially useful when a photographer employs professional models or actors for a special assignment. The use of a flash meter can save hours of valuable time in a commercial studio.

Flash meters are not for professional use alone. They are useful to any photographer. Needless to say, the flash meter eliminates the need for guide number calculations. Whether the lighting is direct or reflected, the flash meter will always give the proper reading.

For portraits, the flash meter must be held near the subject's face.

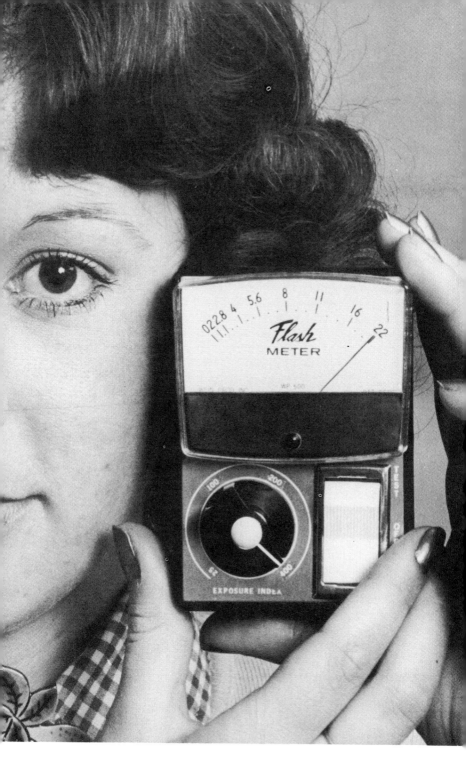

64

Is there any need for an amateur to purchase a powerful flash? For general photography, what do you think of miniflash units priced under $20?

I use nothing but a miniflash myself. I have two electronic flash units at my disposal: a Honeywell Strobonat Auto 770 (with magic eye), which I hardly ever use; and a tiny, much-used Rollei, the actual light part of which is no larger than a postage stamp. The whole unit is no larger than a pack of cigarettes and fits easily into my shirt pocket.

The guide number for Tri-X film at 800 ASA with this miniflash is only 110. There is no need for anything more powerful for shooting at f/11 from a distance of ten feet.

This little device proves most useful in a number of situations, and it goes with me on assignment everywhere. I use it when I need fill light for shooting a backlit subject outdoors, but I use it most often — if not uniquely — for providing indirect lighting. It is too powerful for close-ups. I therefore cover up about half the window with my finger, which leaves a surface of about 1/2" x 3/4" through which the light escapes, and this is with an aperture of f/16.

One distinct advantage of a miniflash is that it runs on "penlight" nickel-cadmium, rechargeable batteries, which are easily obtained anywhere, anytime. I always keep at least half-a-dozen in my equipment bag. Better still, I have recently begun to use a battery charger which is simply plugged into an AC outlet overnight. I start the next morning with "fresh" batteries.

This excellent little flash unit cost about $18, and the recharger about $12 (with batteries). So, good riddance to those large, awkward power packs that we used to have to drag around — as if the poor photographer was not already overloaded!

The Rollei miniflash, smaller than a pack of cigarettes.

On the left, my first choice for colour or black and white, within 10 ft. (3m). I find the other 2 flash units too powerful for 800 ASA black and white film, especially when used as supplementary lighting. They are more appropriate for colour work at medium distances.

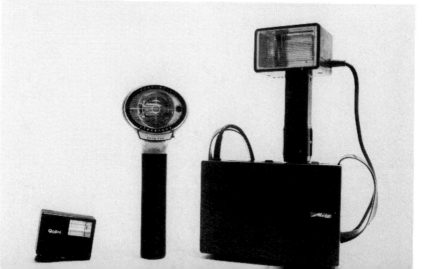

65

What are the advantages and disadvantages of the famous Auto Strobonar electronic flash, which, as the advertisements point out, makes the guide number system unnecessary?

Before examining its advantages and disadvantages, let me just say that this type of electronic flash represents an important innovation in the field of photographic electronics.

It works very simply. There is a small sensor device built into the head of the lamp. This sensor has the ability to monitor the intensity of the light which is emitted by the lamp and reflected from the subject. The sensor automatically increases or decreases the intensity, according to its distance from the subject.

Space will not allow me to go into all the features of this new flash device. The promotional material correctly claims that this type of lighting virtually puts an end to the guide number system and the need to calculate distances for flash. It brings us right into the age of automatic exposures.

There is a scale on the head of the lamp where you must indicate the ASA of the film being used. With the unit switched to automatic, take note of the aperture suggested on the index: the diaphragm will remain at this opening for the duration (Tri-X 400 ASA calls for f/16, for example). If the subject moves or the photographer changes position, the flash unit will make an appropriate adjustment in the strength of the light to assure a good exposure. Moreover, it will do so over a distance of 2 to 23 feet. Since the aperture remains constant at f/16, the flash will obviously throw more light at 20 feet and less at 2 feet. Beyond 23 feet, a manual override takes over from the automatic function, and you must go back to the guide number system.

An important point to note is that the area covered by the sensor is equal to about 12 degrees of the total field covered by the flash itself. In other words, it is fairly easy for the unit to make errors if it has to interpret misleading information.

If, for example, the photographer aims the "eye" towards some darker part of the subject, the flash will overcompensate and the photo will be overexposed. It is therefore best to fix the unit to the camera, so that it is always operating in the same plane as the camera.

Finally, it is interesting to note that the closer the flash is to the subject, the faster it operates. It is capable of turning over at 1/50,000 second. This makes for interesting possibilities in "freezing" action.

The small black eye indicated by the arrow is part of a very refined monitoring system that analyzes the flash unit's own reflected light, independent of distance. The unit should always be aimed directly at the subject, which means you should anchor it to the camera so that it will remain in the same plane.

If the flash is aimed off axis, it will produce a poor exposure.

The right way

The wrong way

66 What does "f/22" mean? Is there a simple answer?

The f/ ... and the accompanying number which appears on the front of all lenses, refers to the ratio between the diameter of the diaphragm (at its widest opening) and the focal length of the lens.

For example: f/2 means the opening of the diaphragm is equal to half the focal length.

If a lens is 2 inches in length, we know immediately that the diameter will be 1 inch. That is, f/2 x 1 = 2 in.

Taking the calculation a little further, we can see that:

f/4 = ¼ of the focal length
f/8 = ⅛ of the focal length
f/11 = 1/11 of the focal length
f/22 = 1/22 of the focal length

This is the focal length divided by the diameter of the diaphragm.

It may be seen from this why telephoto lenses have relatively small apertures (f/8 or f/11), compared to their focal length. A 1000 mm f/2 lens would have to have a diaphragm 500 mm or 20 inches wide — a physical impossibility!

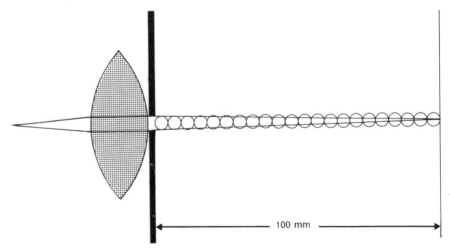

100 mm

If, with this lens, we stop down to f/22, this f/22 represents 1/22nd of the focal length.

Furthermore, it represents a light loss of 22 times over the f/2 aperture.

(Photo by A.D.)

67 Is there a "rule of thumb" by which one can always determine the right exposure, without referring to the instruction sheet or even a light meter?

A light meter is essential in order to achieve photos or slides which are really consistent in terms of contrast and density. However, if you have neither a light meter nor an exposure table, or if you have to work quickly and haven't the time to take careful readings, you need an emergency back-up system.

It is widely acknowledged that lighting conditions in good weather — bright sun, no clouds — are more-or-less the same anywhere in the world. There is, however, a certain difference in the quality of shadows — they are a little harder or blacker in warm countries — because the sun is higher. But the following rule can be safely applied anywhere, during the period from three hours before the sun reaches its zenith to three hours after. The subject should be of a medium tonality.

To get an acceptable exposure at f/16, use a shutter speed equal to the ASA of the film being used.

For example, any photos shot on "X" emulsions, such as Panatomic X, Kodachrome X or Ektachrome X, which are all rated at 64 ASA, will be exposed at 1/60 sec. at f/16. Those of 200 ASA, 1/200 at f/16; those of 500 ASA, 1/500 at f/16; those of 1000 ASA, 1/1000 at f/16.

Of course one should always experiment with other combinations; for example, for 125 ASA, 1/125 at f/16, 1/250 at f/11 or 1/60 at f/22 and so on. The point is to select the shutter speed which corresponds most closely to the ASA.

To be really sure — for there is a certain margin of error here — you should shoot two photos: one half-way between f/11 and f/16, the other half-way between f/16 and f/22.

Always remember that, for very bright scenes which involve snow or sand, you should close down one stop (if you have f/22); if not, use a shutter speed which is one stop faster.

This is an extremely useful rule and applies to colour film as well as to black and white, whether in 35mm, 120mm or plates.

Once again, the subject must be "normally" lit from the front. If there is backlight, open the diaphragm two stops (f/8 rather than f/16).

If in doubt, do not hesitate: use the f/16 aperture and take the ASA rating as the shutter speed. For example, with a 125 ASA film — 1/125 sec. at f/16 (for sunny weather).

68
If I use part of a roll of Tri-X indoors at 1600 ASA, this rating is too high for use outdoors in the wintertime, in clear weather. What can I do to use up a 36-frame roll?

■■■■■■■■■■■■■■■■■■■■■■■■■■■■■

The important thing is to take account of the exposure time indicated by the light meter, so that all the exposures will have roughly the same density.

A rating of 1600 ASA often means having to use a diaphragm/shutter speed combination which exceeds the limits of the camera (1/500 at f/16).

The basic 400 ASA rating of Tri-X film will push many cameras to their limit if the scene involved is especially bright. This requires making up two stops (one to go from 400 ASA to 800 ASA and another from 800 ASA to 1600 ASA). A medium yellow filter will help make up one stop. A light green filter would bring the speed back to 400 ASA, requiring the photographer to close down two stops.

A neutral density filter can be used here to cut down a certain proportion of light entering the camera. Without altering the tone rendering, an ND 4X filter will lower the rating from 1600 to 400 ASA.

An 8X filter can be used in situations where too much depth of field would be undesirable (in a close-up, for example), or where it is necessary to shoot at slow shutter speeds (in order to create a blurred effect).

The ND 2X filter will permit an exposure of 1/500 sec. at f/22, instead of f/32. Thus, an ND 4X, which transmits only 25% of the light, permits opening the diaphragm two stops.

The ND 2X (neutral density) filter reduces the light by 50%. The Sky 1-A filter lets through 100% of the light, but cuts down the blue radiations noticeably.

69 Is it a contradiction to say that colour photos can be shot outdoors after dark with either daylight film or type-B film?

▌■■■■■■■■■■■■■■■■■■■■■■■■■■■■■■■■■▌

There is no real contradiction here. Both of these films will give good results, although of slightly different quality. Colour rendering is a matter of personal taste. There is nothing to prevent an amateur from experimenting with the colour balance in all of his photographs. Other amateurs prefer to stick closely to a faithful rendering of colour — rather than break the rules.

Keep in mind, however, that the two types of emulsion, for daylight and artificial light, are not really balanced for the wide variety of lighting found on any main city street.

If the night street scene is lit with fluorescent tubes, select a daylight film.

Since this is rarely the case, it would be better to use either type A or type B film for artificial light.

A basic characteristic of a photographic emulsion is its ability to store light without limit. For example, astronomers use film emulsions which can be exposed over long periods of time when photographing stars and planets. Although it is possible to take night shots with relatively short exposure times, depending on the sensitivity of the film, the speed of the lens and the lighting conditions; it is nevertheless preferable to work with a tripod. It is best not to exceed a one second exposure with apertures of f/8, f/5.6 and f/4.

The basic exposure for a brightly lit street, with Ektachrome type-B (125 ASA), would be 1/60 at f/2.8. With a tripod, equivalent combinations would be 1/30 at f/4, 1/15 at f/5.6, 1/8 at f/8, 1/2 at f/11 and so on.

Whenever possible, try to shoot at dusk when the sun has disappeared but the sky is still bright enough to make buildings or monuments stand out in relief.

70 Is it possible to shoot using any kind of light whatsoever?

There are two aspects to this question, one technical, the other creative. Let's start with the first. It is true that whenever there is light, there is a theoretical possibility of a photograph. The flame of a candle and the rays of the sun are both capable of forming an image. The difference between them is a quantitative one; the exposure required by candlelight will be approximately 10,000 times longer than that by sunlight. Modern technology has produced **light amplifiers** which can multiply the intensity of a light source by 10,000 to 150,000 times. From a distance of 100 feet, the light of a burning cigarette is enough to light up a surface 100 feet square. You can buy one of these devices for the modest sum of $7,000!

When we turn to the creative side, however, the answer to your question is negative. We often forget that, for the photographer, light constitutes **the basic tool of visual creativity.** In experienced hands, light can develop a child's face with a delicate glow or etch deep lines in an old man's face. It creates the mass of things, parts the layers of a landscape or wipes out any semblance of depth. In the play of shadows and highlights, it draws out surface texture and rhythm. It lends graphic style to a group of elements which would otherwise be of no interest. It can be brash or subtle. It gives an aura of innocence to a woman's body or brings out its latent sensuality. It exposes, it hides. The creative possibilities it offers run the gamut from violence to gentleness, high tension to great calm, restless movement to stasis.

Accordingly, the photographer can and must exercise careful choice of lighting for his subject. This choice depends, on the one hand, on the intrinsic qualities of the subject itself, and on the other, on what the photographer wants to express. He must be guided by his sensibilities. It is important that he establish a special kind of communication between himself and his subject. This will encourage him to bring out the most important features of his subject. It is just as important that he develop an eye for the internal structure of objects, for the lines of force which give strength to a composition.

In the studio the photographer has control over his lighting, but what about outdoors in natural light? Obviously he cannot alter the sun's course, or influence atmospheric conditions. If some event is scheduled to happen at a certain time, like an automobile race for example, the photographer has no other choice but to adapt to those specific conditions. On the other hand, if he is doing a portrait, his choices are considerably greater and he can choose to shoot either in the sun or on an overcast day. The shape and quality of shadows are completely different in late afternoon from what they are at noon. The subject can be directly illuminated by the sun or in the shadows; or, the photographer can use a reflector to soften the shadows in a particular way. In landscape photography, he must exercise patience, because the wait could be long. He must choose a certain moment in the day, decide what sort of weather is most appropriate and deal with the transformations w h i c h occur from one season to the next.

These few examples indicate the care with which a photographer must select his lighting.

Lateral lighting throws
the textures into relief.

This lighting accentuates the
plastic qualities of the nude.

One way to shoot backlighting.

Another use of backlighting,
to give a rhythm of light and
shade to the angles of
doors and windows.

The sombre light of this winter day suits the desolation of the scene perfectly.

The sun seems to be shining from deep beneath the water.

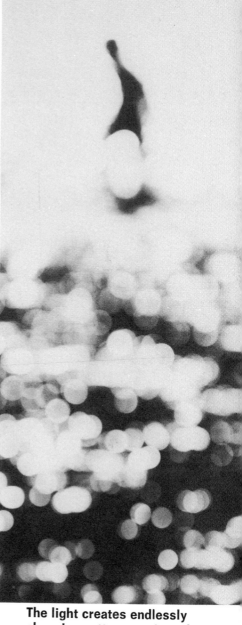

The light creates endlessly changing patterns as it strikes waves by the seashore.

71 What are the most important things to know about the visual qualities of lighting?

With lighting, visual impact depends upon two factors: the incident angle and direction of the light, and the degree to which it is diffused or concentrated.

These two factors determine the form of the shadows. The higher the light source above the camera, the longer the shadows will be. To each subject there corresponds an optimum height for the light source, one which will present the subject in an effective way. This is accomplished by a careful handling of both shadows and highlights. Unfortunately, shadow effects on other objects and on the background are often overlooked when the main subject gets too much attention.

In general, lighting situated below the level of the camera is rarely necessary. Such lighting creates strange effects and models the face in a very unflattering way. Not surprisingly, it is used quite often in horror films.

Vertical alteration of the main light source creates one set of effects, horizontal changes of position offer another. Theoretically, the light source can be placed anywhere in relation to the subject. In practice, especially for portrait photography, the subject is usually lit from the front and the side, at an angle of about 45 degrees. Backlighting has an especially pleasing quality and can be used in conjunction with many different subjects, but is at its best in the landscape. It surrounds objects with a luminous glow, gives them depth and shines through transparent objects to create warm, diffuse patches of light.

Just as important as the shape of the shadows is their degree of outline. This is a major consideration when building a certain kind of **atmosphere.** A hard, deliberate shadow suggests strength, tension or movement. A soft shadow, on the other hand, suggests tenderness, joy or youth.

The photographer controls this effect by carefully selecting his lighting. The sun tends to create very hard shadows, particularly around noon; in the studio, the **spotlight** acts in a similar way. Parabolic reflectors create a measure of diffusion. Diffused light can be considerably increased by placing a diffusion screen made of plastic or fibreglass in front of the lamp. You can maximize the diffusion by using nothing but **reflected light:** instead of aiming the light source directly at the subject, shine it on a white screen. The screen, in turn, reflects the light in a pleasantly subtle, diffuse way. Outdoors, hazy weather or an overcast sky will produce much the same effect.

Diffusion of the light gives a very delicate quality to this young girl's face.

The spot throws a hard light that can model the human face in an infinite variety of ways.

72 How can I assemble an effective lighting system in my studio?

■ I

Every generation of photographers has had its fashions and its taboos in lighting. Basically, any lighting set-up which is well matched to the subject is valid.

There are two general principles of lighting. Once you have an idea of what kind of ambience you want to create, these principles will prove to be indispensible aids. (See Question 71)

a) The vertical lighting principle

The main light source is almost always placed above the camera. In the preceeding question we noted that lighting placed below the height of the camera rarely gives a pleasing effect. Man has always been used to seeing the outside world lit by the sun, which, of course, throws shadows down, not up. This may at first seem a trivial observation; but in fact, it demonstrates how we have been significantly conditioned in the way we see. A very simple but striking example is displayed on the next page. These two photos show two surfaces, one of which seems to be raised in relief, the other carved hollow. In fact, they are two photos of the same surface, but with one photo turned around. The brain assumes that the shadow was created by light from above; this makes the relief look inverted. The reader can see this for himself by turning the book upside down; the inversion then reverses itself, the relief becoming hollow and vice versa.

b) The principle of single-source lighting

The eye requires that a lighting set-up give the **impression** that there is only one source of light, and thereby **only one set of shadows.** A photograph will have much more cohesion and impact if it is modelled by shadows derived from only one light source. This is a particular problem, of course, for the studio. This principle, like the first one, is based on how we have been conditioned by sunlight — a single shadow effect.

A studio lighting set-up might require any number of lamps; each lamp plays a definite part in creating the over-all effect. The main lighting source is known as the **key light.** The selection and positioning of this light is crucial, because it must create the general ambience and establish the main shadow effects. **Any additional lamps must be considered subordinate to the key light.**

Occasionally you may consider that the key light is sufficient and be tempted to shoot without any other lighting. With a single light source you will find that the shadows are completely black and devoid of detail. This is because the relationship between the light zones and the dark zones (the **brightness range of the subject**) is too great to allow the emulsion to register details inside the two zones. In most cases, a second lamp or **fill light** is needed. Sometimes a simple reflector made of white cardboard will do. Its purpose is to open up and to brighten the main shadows. In order to prevent it from creating another set of shadows, this light is usually placed in line with the optical axis of the camera. The closer it is to the subject, the lighter the shadows, and vice versa.

A third group of lamps is used to create highlights (hair, outlines, etc.), and to give more body or impact to a composition.

Finally, the background should be:

a) well recessed from the subject so that unwanted shadows thrown by the subject do not appear, and

b) lit independently of the main subject so that its tonality (light or dark) can be modulated to harmonize with the over-all ambience.

The brain automatically assumes that shadow effects are created by a light source situated above the subject. That is why in one of these photographs the relief seems to be hollowed out. The illusion is inverted if you turn the book upside down.

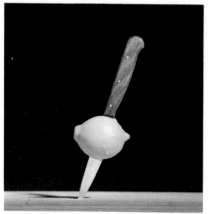

a) normal

c) green

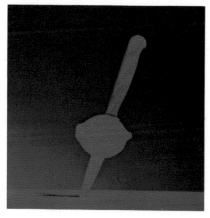

b) red

d) blue

A lemon under 4 different
kinds of lighting:

Plate 9

A blue colour cast typical of a scene lit only by blue sky —
Marseille, late afternoon

Plate 10

Regular shot on Kodachrome II

A green .30CC filter was used
to give better saturation
of the greens

Shot with a yellow
.30CC filter

Plate 11

Lighting with a 60 and a 150 W bulb. A colour temperature of less than 3200° K gives a very warm tone to the wood. (Ektachrome H.S.B.)

Plate 12

Type-B film used at mid-day
gives very cold tones.
Underexposing 1 stop
reinforces the effect

Photo taken at sunset
on Kodachrome II

Type-B film. Front lighting,
3200° K. The blue cast
is caused by the use
of electronic flash

Type-B film at sunset. The orange
colour cast is eliminated and
the rendering is quite natural

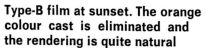

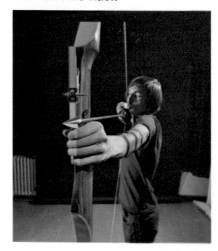

Plate 13

a) The original subject

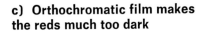

b) Panchromatic film gives an acceptable tonal balance

c) Orthochromatic film makes the reds much too dark

d) A non-chromatic emulsion gives a false rendering to almost all the original colours

Plate 14

The Kodak 1-A Skylight filter

Without the filter

Plate 15

**Photos shot with the special
Micro Nikkor lens**

Plate 16

Too many shadows interfere with one another and weaken the over-all impact.

A single, strong shadow effect gives the picture unity and cohesion

73 I like shooting black and white photos in overcast weather or in snowstorms. Is there any way to achieve an extra degree of contrast?

■■■■■■■■■■■■■■■■■■■■■■■■■■■■■■■■

This kind of photographic exercise requires that you overstep the basic rules of photography (clear sky, fine weather, etc.).

The following advice will produce pictures worthy of being exhibited. It is very simple: underexpose one stop, occasionally two, then increase your developing time by at least a third or more. For example, if the recommended developing time is six minutes, increase it to nine minutes and agitate **briskly** every 30 seconds.

To get even more contrast, print your photos on #4, #5 or even #6 paper (Agfa Gevaert), and you will notice a marked improvement in the whites and blacks.

This technique does not, of course, apply to colour, nor does the use of contrast filters (yellow, green, red) make an appreciable difference.

The Aurora Borealis is difficult to photograph because it has little inherent contrast and requires a rather long exposure. This picture was taken with the camera lying on the ground facing straight up. Tri-X, ½ sec., f/4.5.

The Aurora Borealis is in
constant motion, which results
in blurring and poor contrast.
This calls for printing on
Brovira No. 6. The same holds
for shooting in fog
or a snowstorm.

74

At certain times of day, there is a considerable drop in the AC line voltage in my studio; to what extent might this affect colour rendering?

More electricity is generally consumed in the evening than during the day, although the noticeable difference is minimal.

A drop in line voltage definitely has an effect on the colour temperature of 3400°K photoflood lamps and 3200°K tungsten lamps.

Colour temperature is a function of a particular voltage.

Remember that 10 volts equals 100°K.

A drop in voltage of 20 V would lower the colour temperature of a 3400°K. photoflood to 3200°K., and so on.

We know that, if we lower the colour temperature, the colour rendering will be hotter, and to re-balance it we would have to raise the temperature with a correcting filter.

The 82 series correcting filters (blue, cooling) would be a solution. Use a darker or lighter tint, depending on the degree of correction required. (See Question 2)

If this has been a serious problem for you, you should get a **voltage regulator.** All the large retailers have them. You might also limit your shooting to those times of day or night when the use of lighting and electrical appliances is at its lowest.

Reflex camera, 105mm lens, 1/1000 sec., at f/16. Printed on Brovira No. 4.

75 Would it not be better to use just one kind of film for both colour and black and white, and thereby eliminate all unnecessary conversion filters and complicated charts?

You would have much to gain by diversifying your resources, especially in colour, where differences from one emulsion to another are so visible. The colour rendering of one emulsion might bring out those subtleties which black and white is just not capable of producing. Certain black and white emulsions do, however, offer the advantage of greater speed and sharper contrast.

A high-speed colour emulsion (Kodak High Speed Ektachrome, 160 ASA, for example) will give pale pastel tones. At the other extreme, saturation will be very high with a film whose sensitivity rating is low (Kodachrome II, 25 ASA, for example, which is well known for its contrasty colour). By knowing the qualities of each of these emulsions, you can select the film which best suits a particular lighting situation. In the absence of brilliant sunshine,

I personally prefer to use Agfachrome, Anscochrome or Ektachrome X. In clear weather I prefer slower films like Kodachrome II and X. With overcast skies, or at sunrise or sunset, my camera would be loaded with a fast film like High Speed Ektachrome or Anscochrome 500 (GAF), in order to shoot at fast shutter speeds.

However, all of this is no more than a question of taste. You should experiment with all kinds of films, both outdoors and in, to find which films suit your purposes best.

If you use the same emulsion (especially colour), when you move from indoors to outdoors or vice versa you will still need a conversion filter. If, however, you always use an electronic flash when you work indoors, you **can** stick to the same type of film.

But sooner or later, when you compare your photos with those of your friends, you will realize that flash isn't everything. The way a flash lights a subject from straight on is invariably dull and flat. I have little doubt that you will soon be tempted to experiment with your own lighting.

In the table on the following page, you will note that there are really only four conversion filters in current use. If you fix your shooting according to a certain kind of lighting, say 3400°K photofloods, you will have a whole range of colour emulsions to choose from — and this table is far from complete. The 80B filter will give you very good results indoors. By adding the 85B filter, you convert this film into a daylight emulsion for outdoor shooting.

Table on the following page.

(Photo by A.D.)

EXPOSURE TABLE FOR VARIOUS
COLOUR FILMS

	Film Type	Light Source	ASA and Conversion Filters			Format	Processing
			Day	Photo-flood	Tungsten (3200° K)		
For Printing	Kadocolor-X		80	25 #80B	20 #80A	120 135-126	
	Ektacolor professionnel †types (6101)		100	32 #80B	25 #80A	135 et 120	C-22
	Ektacolor profestype L		64 #85‡	64 #81A§	64¶		
For Slides	Kodachrome II		25	8 #80B	6 #80A	135 828	Toronto 15 Ontario
	Kodachrome-X		64	20 #80B	16 #80A	135-126	Toronto 15 Ontario
	Agfachrome CT-18		50	20 #80B	15 #80C	135 120 127	Agfa-chrome Service 33 Gurney Crescent Toronto 9 Ontario
	Ektachrome-X		64	20 #80B	16 #80A	120 135-126	E-4
	GAF Ansochrome		64	32 #80B	16 80B + 82A	135	
	High Speed Ektachrome		160	50- #80B	40— #80A	135 126	E-4
			400*	125- #80B*	100— #80A*		
	GAF Ansochrome		100	50 #80B	40 #80A	135	
	GAF Ansochrome		200	100 #80B	80 #80A	135	
	GAF Ansochrome (500)		500	250 #80B	125 #80A	135	
	Kodachrome II professional type A		25 #85B	40	32 #82A	135	Toronto 15 Ontario
	Kodak High Speed Ektachrome (Tungsten)		80 #85B	100 #81A	125	120 135	E-4
			200* #85B	250 #81A	320		
	GAF Anchrochrome (Tungsten 100)		64 #85B	80 #81A	100	135	
			200 #85B	225 #81A	300		

* It is possible (although not necessarily desirable) to push these films to 2½ times their original rating, but you must advise the commercial lab of this, or follow the appropriate instruction if you develop at home.
† Exposure time should be 1/10 sec. or less.
‡ For exposure of 1/10 sec.
§ For exposure of 1 sec.
¶ For exposure of 5 sec.

(Photo by A.D.)

U.S. STEEL
G. du Tonkin
Kioungtchéou
I. Haïnan
Donghoi
Hue
Tourane
Iles Paracels
Quangngai
Quinhon
MER DE
VIET-NAM
C Padaran
Is. Calamianes
CHINE
Palaouan
P. Condore
Détr. de Balabac
MÉRIDIONALE
Jesselton

76 When I work with an electronic flash, how do I eliminate the greenish cast produced by fluorescent lighting?

You are working at too slow a shutter speed and are thus letting in too much of the ambient light.

Generally, synchronization for electronic flash (with a focal plane shutter) is set at 1/30 or 1/60 sec., which means that, at relatively large apertures (f/4 or f/5.6), a good deal of light from the fluorescent source will get by. Hence, a greenish cast results.

To remedy this, you should increase the shutter speed to 1/125 sec., if your camera will allow. If not, exchange your camera (a rather drastic solution) for one with a diaphragm shutter which allows synchronization up to 1/500 sec. Turn out the fluorescent lights before you start shooting. Or perhaps you could use a more powerful electronic flash. This would enable you to stop down two stops and avoid the ambient light.

Apart from these suggestions, you have only two other choices.

a) CC (colour correction) filters. Once you know the type of florescent lighting involved, you can use the appropriate filter (CC 10M or CC 10Y). It is much better to use negative colour film for this kind of shooting because the colour can be balanced when you print.

b) The new FL-B and FL-D filters (for type-B and daylight film respectively). Both are manufactured specifically to control this green cast and give very good results. Opening up one stop is advisable for both.

Reversible daylight film used under fluorescent bulbs (cool white or warm white) also usually gives a green cast. It is best to do some tests with CC (M or Y) filters. When you find the right one, you can insert it right into the slide holder and leave it there permanently. These filters come in the form of very thin gels.

77

Even though a solar eclipse occurs infrequently, how can it be most easily photographed?

■ I

There are a few but important rules to follow in photographing an eclipse of the sun. (The accompanying photos were taken during the eclipse of March 7, 1970.)

You will hear about an eclipse well in advance from the newspapers. Because an entire eclipse lasts only an hour or so, you must be well prepared.

There is one basic and **absolute** precaution: never, for any reason whatsoever, look directly at the sun with the naked eye.

Expose three sheets of 4 x 5 in. film to daylight and develop them normally. You will be able to look at the sun through these sheets of film, or else through the view-finder of the camera, after you have placed the sheets in front of the lens.

You should appreciate that, because it is the sun you are photographing, you will have to reduce its intensity at least 10,000 times to the intensity of an ordinary distant star.

To do so, you will of course have to "look" at it, if only for the focussing and framing.

Shoot with an ND 5.00 neutral density filter, or else two No. 1 filters (ND 3.00 and ND 2.00), which will let only 1/1000 of 1% of the solar light pass and will give a very dark sky.

If you decide to shoot only one or two photos on different negatives, remember that the exposure time will vary with the extent of the eclipse.

The approximate exposure for a partial eclipse, with, say, 25% of the sun obscured, would be f/11 at 1/125 sec., for a 160 ASA film and a 5.00 filter.

Do not at any point remove the ND filter. Instead, increase the exposure time as necessary (see the following table). In the case of a total eclipse (which is quite rare), you could remove the filter.

Remember that the final phase of the eclipse lasts no more than two minutes. If you want to shoot a series of photos on the one negative, you will have to do it fairly quickly — no more than ten seconds between shots.

Needless to say, sequential shooting requires the use of a tripod. Be sure your camera is equipped to do double exposures.

For individual photos, it is best to use a telephoto of at least 200mm, which will capture the sun (and the moon in silhouette) in acceptable proportions.

The ideal lens for sequential shooting is undoubtedly the 85 mm, which will give a series of 10 to 12 photos of the sun (one roughly every 5 minutes), all on the same negative.

Make your calculations several hours in advance of the eclipse, to be sure you know what the position of the sun will be over a period of about an hour.

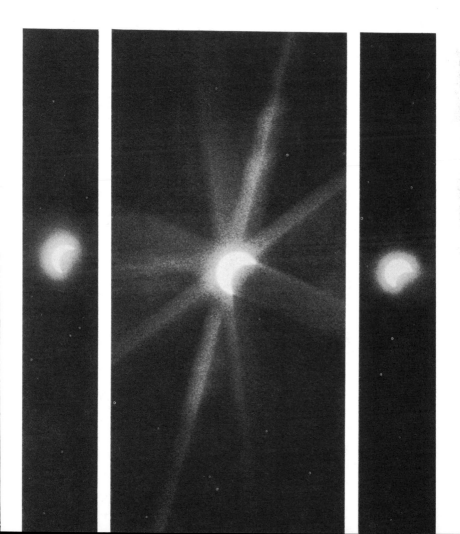

SHOOTING A SOLAR ECLIPSE

Table of Approximate Exposures

Film Speed & Other Data	1 S.C.	1 CIN.	2 S.C.	2 CIN.	3 S.C.	3 CIN.	4 S.C.	4 CIN.
ASA 25-32	f/5.6	f/11	f/4.5	f/8	f/4.5	f/2.8	f/4.5	f/1.4
Aperture N.D.	5.00	5.00	—	—	—	—	—	—
Filter Speed	1/100	16 I.S.	1/100	16 I.S.	1/10	16 I.S.	1/2	16 I.S.
ASA 40-50	f/6.3	f/13	f/5.6	f/11	f/5.6	f/3.5	f/5.6	f/1.9
Aperture N.D.	5.00	5.00	—	—	—	—	—	—
Filter Speed	1/100	16 I.S.	1/100	16 I.S.	1/10	16 I.S.	1/2	16 I.S.
ASA 64-80	f/8	f/16	f/6.3	f/13	f/6.3	f/4	f/6.3	f/2
Aperture N.D.	5.00	5.00	—	—	—	—	—	—
Filter Speed	1/100	16 I.S.	1/100	16 I.S.	1/10	16 I.S.	1/2	16 I.S.
ASA 125-160	f/11	f/22	f/8	f/16	f/8	f/4.5	f/8	f/2
Aperture N.D.	5.00	5.00	—	—	—	—	—	—
Filter Speed	1/100	16 I.S.	1/100	16 I.S.	1/10	16 I.S.	1/2	16 I.S.
ASA 200-250	f/16	f/9.5	f/11	f/22	f/11	/6.3	f/11	f/2.8
Aperture N.D.	5.00	6.00	—	—	—	—	—	—
Filter Speed	1/100	16 I.S.	1/100	16 I.S.	1/10	16 I.S.	1/2	16 I.S.
ASA 400-650	f/22	f/11	f/16	f/11	f/16	f/9.5	f/16	f/4
Aperture N.D.	5.00	6.00	—	1.00	—	—	—	—
Filter Speed	1/100	16 I.S.	1/100	16 I.S.	1/10	16 I.S.	1/2	16 I.S.
ASA 1250	f/32	f/18	f/22	f/16	f/22	f/13	f/22	f/5.6
Aperture N.D.	5.00	6.00	—	1.00	—	—	—	—
Filter Speed	1/100	16 I.S.	1/100	16 I.S.	1/10	16 I.S.	1/2	16 I.S.

1 = Partial
2 = Total (prominences)
3 = Total (corona int.)
4 = Total (corona ext.)

F.S. = Frames per second
S.C. = Still camera
CIN. = Cine camera

(Photo by A.D.) ➤

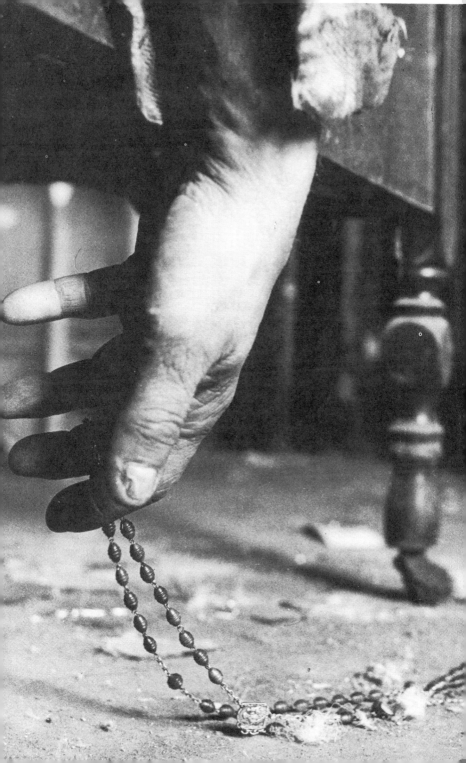

Could you suggest an approach for shooting reflected images?

There are reflections everywhere. We are surrounded by surfaces which create reflections, running from the unusual to the surreal.

There are too many reflective surfaces to categorize them all. To suggest a few: puddles, store windows, glass counter tops in stores and restaurants, glass high-rise building fronts, glass doors, polished floors, concrete or asphalt roads after a rain, door-knobs, toasters and electric household appliances, automobile hub-caps, every chromed surface imaginable, smoked glass or mirrors, oily surfaces, still water, camera lens elements, and so on.

The possibilities for a creative photographer are limited only by his imagination. Perhaps it is just because there are so many possibilities that we overlook reflections as subjects for photography. But don't make the mistake of using a polarizing filter. It is designed precisely to eliminate reflections, whereas the idea is to discover them and create a new experience. To photograph a reflection simply for the sake of reproducing it will not give a very interesting result. Try to catch the reflection at an unexpected angle.

Here is a challenge that beginners should take on: photograph only reflections for a whole week. You will be amazed at how this stimulates the imagination. Such an exercise helps the beginner to develop his talent almost without realizing it. Forget about the aesthetics or philosophical implications of a reflection. These do not matter. What does matter is you. If you are taken with a particular reflection, shoot it. But think a little before you press the shutter to make that picture a part of you.

The Chateau Laurier, Ottawa, reflected in a restaurant window.

A seminary in Quebec City reflected in a puddle.

Reflection in a mirrowed column, from 12 ft. (4 m).

79   Why do the subjects which I see and shoot seem more attractive, more captivating, than the actual photographs?

Quite simply, you have confused the way **you** see with the way your **lens** sees. In other words, you have not had enough experience yet to **"see" in photographic terms.** Everyone knows that the camera lens is constructed along the same lines as the human eye. But it is unrealistic, not to say naive, to believe that two things which are structurally identical must function in an identical fashion. It's just not so.

The camera has only one "eye". It is like a colour-blind cyclops! It cannot interpret anything; it "looks" without "seeing". It is objective in an absolute sense. Your camera has neither soul nor intelligence. It is a mere piece of machinery that works according to the laws of chemistry and optics. The human eye, which is seeing in colour and in three dimensions, has great interpretive powers.

If you were accustomed to looking at or analyzing a scene with **one eye closed,** you would be one step closer to optical reality.

Since the eye is selective, it sees only one part of one scene at one time. In photography, on the other hand, we use lenses that vary the angle of view from 1° to 180 degrees. This is to say nothing of the focussing and depth of field factors, which would take us into problems beyond the scope of this book.

There is an additional discrepancy between the eye and the lens: an emulsion is able to render visible what is invisible to the human eye as in night and astronomical photography.

In order to think in terms of the eye of a camera, you must be familiar with the theories of "optical perspective", as well as the capacities and limits of your lenses. I strongly recommend that you refer to the chapter on "visual language" in my book **Techniques In Photography.**

To duplicate what the camera
sees with its one eye,
you must cover one of your
own. We see stereoscopically,
the camera does not.

But the best thing is simply
to look through the lens
with one eye closed.

80

The way you hold your camera seems to depend on whether you are working with a wide-angle or a telephoto. How should the camera be held?

There is unanimous agreement that a majority of ruined photos, apart from those that have been under or overexposed, are caused by a poor grip on the camera. Mishandling of the camera invariably produces shaky photos when the shutter is released.

Chances are that this will not happen while shooting with a wide-angle lens, but as the focal length increases, use of a tripod becomes necessary.

The shutter release is located in the same place on almost all 35mm cameras. The right hand operates the release, while the left takes care of focussing and aperture. In other words, the correct way to hold a camera applies equally to all 35mm cameras. Do not forget that the strap must be wrapped around the right wrist for two important reasons:

a) to prevent the camera from falling if you lose your grip;

b) to prevent the strap from appearing unexpectedly in front of the lens.

Study closely each of the photos illustrating this article. They demonstrate better than words that the arm can be used as a tripod; it is only the shutter release finger which is not kept tense.

Thus, try to become one with the camera; to transform yourself into a sort of tripod with elbows and legs firmly planted. If the camera is well supported there will be no room for vibrations when the shutter is released. The photographer's forehead provides additional cushion support for the camera.

These points apply only to hand-held shooting. For more details on shooting at slow shutter speeds, see Question 98.

Incidentally, there is a general rule worth remembering: the shutter speed must be at least equal to the focal length of the lens being used. For example: with a 200mm, you need a shutter speed of at least 1/200 sec.; with a 500mm, 1/500 sec., etc.

Hold the right arm at right angles to the left, press the camera against your forehead, and release the shutter very gently.

Shooting horizontally, with your left elbow planted firmly on your left knee. This is an ideal position for telephotos.

How to shoot in the midst of a crowd.

Hold the camera pressed firmly against your chest.

Pulling against the strap helps steady the camera.

81

What is a "composite" photo and can this concept be applied to portraits?

A "composite" is a series of photos of a subject taken from different angles and then arranged in a certain way on a sheet of paper or piece of cardboard. Those shots which are most important can be blown up a bit more than the others so that the whole arrangement can be taken in at a glance.

This technique is ideally suited to the portrait (see photos opposite). In this composite you can see how much more is revealed of the little animal than could be in just one or two photos. One photo may present its message quite well, but it can only show us one aspect of the subject in question.

Any girl who hopes to become a professional model would do well to have a few "composite" photos to show prospective employers. One should be a large close-up, another three-quarter length and a third full length.

The photos can be easily mounted with Dry Mounting Tissue, a very thin paper that can be cut to the exact dimensions of the photo before it is "melted" under the pressure of a hot iron.

As a last reminder, never place a hot iron directly on a photo emulsion. Use a piece of wrapping paper over it to prevent damage.

Ruby's first weekend at the cottage.

82 Do you have any special advice for taking pictures at the zoo?

■ ■

Try to photograph the animals in such a way that they seem to be in their natural environment. If possible, work with a telephoto of at least 135mm.

In most zoos, the animals are kept behind protective barriers. If you get close enough, you can overcome this problem by shooting between the bars, but be sure not to get any closer than the zoo regulations allow. The dangerous animals are always kept behind a double enclosure, which you should never try to pass. Two or three fatal accidents have happened at zoos when over-zealous photographers have managed to get too close!

To recreate the proper setting, try to shoot into a background of foliage. You can sometimes make the cages disappear from your shot simply by ensuring that the metalwork is out of focus.

You will soon discover how easy it is to photograph wild animals in captivity, because they tend to be very docile and easy to shoot in close-up.

No particular lighting is called for, although I think photos taken in cloudy weather are better than those taken in bright sunlight. The techniques of portrait photography apply pretty well here.

Your major problem will be a certain lack of communication with the subject! ... Be patient, keep your wits about you, anticipate the animals' moves and do all you can to eliminate "civilization" from your pictures by cropping tightly when you come to print.

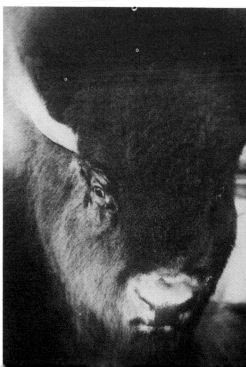

83 How can I take close-ups if I cannot get physically closer than 10 feet?

Contrary to popular belief, you do not have to get close to a subject to shoot a close-up.

Indeed, it is often necessary to use a telephoto lens to avoid throwing a shadow on the subject, from either the camera or the photographer's body. The telephoto should also be used if the subject is inaccessible or too nervous to be approached (in the case of an animal for example).

It is a paradoxial but well-founded principle that in optics the further away you move from the subject the more closely you see.

If you place a 3X tripler between the camera and a 200mm lens, you will get a 600mm lens, which will enable you to frame about 5 in. of the subject on 35mm film, at a distance of over 12 feet.

Results will be excellent with a doubler or tripler of good quality, providing you keep in mind the special measures that have been taken with these lenses. You must stop down a good deal, avoid the slightest vibration and compensate for the loss of light. (See Question 48)

The telephoto approach also eliminates the risk of distortion. Distortion occurs with the use of a close-up lens at a short distance from the subject, particularly if the axis of the lens is slightly out of line.

**Photo shot from 12 ft.
with a 500mm
catadioptric lens.**

84 What rules must be followed to obtain first-class aerial photographs? What is the cost involved?

■ I

Aerial photography is relatively expensive, but it can be very profitable.

First of all, you must rent a small airplane or helicopter, which costs between $50 and $80 an hour. Accordingly, you should plan your time very carefully before the flight: colour film, black and white film, orange filter, etc. and the sites to be photographed. You should plan to work from an altitude between 800 and 1500 feet. Over populated areas airplanes are usually not permitted to fly under 1000 feet.

At moderate altitudes, the ideal lens for a 35mm camera is a standard 55mm, although an 85mm can prove very useful for closer shots.

Try to avoid shooting through a window. Arrange with the pilot to have the door removed or the window left open.

Whether you shoot from a plane or a helicopter, the most serious problem is vibration. It is best to do your shooting at 1/1000 sec. and to avoid leaning against the cabin wall.

There are many types of 2-3- and 4-seater planes, but as far as photography is concerned, the best one is the Piper Cub. The placement of its wings offers minimal obstruction of the view. The cruising speed of this kind of plane is about 125 mph, but for shooting purposes it can be slowed down to 50 or even 40 mph.

Although 35mm will give perfectly good results there is no doubt that you get the best results in aerial photography with larger format cameras — 4 x 5, or 2¼ x 2¼. Apart from their great mobility, they permit the use of a fairly grainy film.

If you are shooting an area which is fairly flat, there is no problem with depth of field. You can therefore use the fastest shutter speed possible.

The best time to shoot is during mid-morning and mid-afternoon when the rays of the sun are sloping at a 45° angle. This lends a modelling effect.

The cost? Apart from the rental fees, the client pays about $35 for the first photo. The cost of any additional photos is reduced in proportion to the number ordered. Should you manage to sell aerial work to a client who has not commissioned it, the first photo should be sold for at least $25. If your clients find

your prices a bit steep, just re-
mind them of the high cost of
the "tripod" you had to rent! . . .

85 Are there any tricks for making a photo seem sharp, even though it really isn't?

The best way to assure a sharp picture at all times is to use the fastest possible shutter speed and the optimum aperture (which is neither wide open nor stopped right down).

Refer to Question 45 in order to understand the significance of this last point.

Whenever you have the choice of photographing at a fast shutter speed and wide aperture, or at a slow shutter speed and minimal aperture, I strongly recommend that you always opt for the fast shutter speed. A wide aperture does not, of course, assure as sharp an image as a smaller aperture, but the shutter speed is of much greater importance here than any aperture.

One always wonders (especially when working in available light) whether it is better to have a slightly fuzzy picture (due to movement of the camera or the subject at slow shutter speeds), or a picture that **lacks depth of field** (wide aperture, fast shutter speed). The second option will give a picture that looks sharper than it really is. In the first case there will be more depth of field, but there will seem to be less sharpness over all.

You will therefore do best to work with a practically non-existent depth of field by stopping down to f/1.4 or f/2.8.

It has often been said that a portrait is acceptable when the subject's eyes are in focus, even if the nose or ears are way out of focus. Focussing sharply on one part of your subject will give an illusion of sharpness to the whole picture.

Remember that a narrow aperture may increase the depth of field, but adds nothing to the sharpness of any part of the picture which is already in focus. Indeed, it tends to detract from the sharpness of the picture as a whole

Never try to enlarge a detail or portion of a negative which is not sharp.

None of this is new, of course: it all stems from fundamental rules of photographic practice. In addition, you should remember to have a pale subject against a dark background and vice versa, in order to heighten the effect of sharpness. The subject and the background should always contrast with each other.

Any foreground or background matter which is out of focus should be sharpened whenever it will help make the subject stand out.

One last trick is to print on paper that is more contrasty than usual. If you look at two prints side by side, the one on matte paper, the other on glossy, you will see that the glossy print is more contrasty and therefore sharper.

Standard 50mm lens — 1/1000 sec. at f/2.8. The area which is in focus is small, but the picture is quite acceptable.

The slow shutter speed has caused a slight blurring.

Printed on a high contrast paper, the photo appears to be sharper.

86 How do you make black and white slides from a black and white photograph?

There are two ways to do it. The first is to load your camera with a roll of Panatomic X, a very fine grain film which is ideal for copy photography. I assume that you have through-the-lens metering. Set the film speed at 25 ASA. If you have a 35mm (wide-angle) lens, it will be easy for you to shoot photos bigger than 5 x 7 without a close-up lens. With a 52mm (standard) lens, you should use a close-up lens for shooting the smaller formats.

In order to save time and take advantage of fairly uniform light conditions, you would be well advised to work outdoors, when the sun's rays are falling at roughly a 45° angle. If you are shooting glossy photos, watch out for reflections. The best way to calculate your exposure is to use the **18% neutral density card** (for reflected light, obviously). Then you are ready to go. Do your shooting as you would for any other subject. Just be sure to fill up the frame.

One advisable precaution would be to double up on your exposures. If the meter suggests an aperture of f/8, shoot one exposure between f/8 and f/11 and another between f/8 and f/5.6, so that one is sure to turn out. Remember that no light meter is perfect, and since you cannot make corrections in the darkroom, you must be sure to get a perfect exposure.

Next, get a Kodak Direct Positive Film Developing Kit, which should be used according to the following table:

At 68°F:

first developer	8 min.
wash	2 min.
bleach	1 min.
clearing bath	2 min.
redeveloper	4 min.
rinse	1 min.
fixer	5 min.
final wash	10 min.

After drying, you can get on with the mounting.

For those who do not have a darkroom there is a second method. Shoot in the same way as for the first method, but use a daylight colour film. When your film is returned from the lab, you will be surprised to see a set of fine black and white slides on colour film.

I might add that this method is the easiest, fastest and most economical, and one which professionals often use. It is straightforward and trouble-free. Remember that when shooting with colour film you should shoot as close to noon as possible, to avoid any chance of getting an unwanted colour cast.

The best method for making black and white slides is also the easiest: use Ektachrome X and shoot outdoors in the sun.

87 Why is my film always underexposed when I shoot in a large room (like a gym), even though I follow the guide number?

■ ■

A guide number does not cover all situations. It is valid for purposes of shooting in a medium-sized room, where there is a certain degree of light reflected from walls and ceiling.

When you find yourself in a very large interior, the normal light loss will be about 50%. With the walls and ceiling far away, only the subject itself will reflect any light (even if the walls and ceil-ing are not dark). It then becomes necessary to open up 2 or 3 stops. This will also help lighten a dark background.

It is best to make a few tests, especially if you shoot often in a particular place. Vary your exposure by one stop each time you shoot until you arrive at a new guide number for that particular room.

Photo taken at 15 ft. at f/4 (no reflecting surface). Indoor, f/8 would have done.

Photo taken without reflecting surface at between f/8 and f/5.6.

88 With the exception of a telephoto lens, is there some way of photographing people without their knowing it?

■ ■

Although they are very difficult to find, you can try to get a Cir-co-Mirrotack. This device is a tube three to four inches in length which contains a mirror that can be moved 45° in any direction. It can be fitted to almost any camera with the help of an appropriate adaptor and costs between $15 and $20.

With your camera pointed straight in front of you, you can photograph a subject to the left, the right, above or below you. You simply adjust the tube for the desired angle.

This is not an indispensable piece of equipment, but it will allow you to shoot people who would otherwise not allow themselves to be photographed. If they see your camera, they will think you are shooting something else and remain relaxed and natural.

There is nothing like a camera for putting some people out of sorts. You cannot stop life for your camera: if embarrassment overtakes your subject, your photograph will probably lose its impact.

There is only one stumbling block: you will have to practise your aim for some time before you master the framing problem. Remember that with a mirror all movements are reversed; correct to the left when you want to correct to the right, up when you want to correct down, and so forth. Good luck!

Here is a gadget that is very popular with policemen and private detectives — a mirror adaptor. It allows you to shoot without aiming the camera at the subject. Suitable only for Takumar lenses (200mm — f/3.5, SMC 200mm — f/4, and 300mm — f/6.3 Tele-Takumar).

Could anyone look more natural?

Nobody but you . . .

89 How can I superimpose a moon or a sun on my pictures?

∎ ■ ∎

The superimposition of a moon or a sun is not very difficult.

Quite recently, I shot three 20-frame rolls of colour film entirely of the moon. It was a nice evening, and I settled down on my balcony, camera on tripod (with a 500mm lens on the camera), and waited for "moonrise".

Before shooting, I removed the lens, opened the shutter by means of the "B" exposure device and made a pencil mark on the film inside the camera. This served to mark the beginning of the film for later, when I want to superimpose other photos on this roll. I can be certain that my moons are always in the correct spot.

It is important for all the moons to be in the same spot, that is, in the upper right corner for horizontal shots, and in the upper left corner for vertical shots. In either case it is absolutely necessary for them to be in the upper half of the frame.

Later you can simply store the exposed film in the refrigerator.

The exposure for black and white should be as fast as possible because of the possibility of vibration with the telephoto.

Exposure for a **full moon** is much the same as it would be for regular daytime shooting.

You can stock up on sun exposures too. For black and white, you need a very dark red filter like the Kodak Wratten 29F. Shoot placing the sun in a certain position in the frame . . . and remember where it was. The filter will make the sky virtually black; the sun will stand out against the sky and facilitate superimpression later on in the darkroom. Just be sure, when you select a landscape or other scene for your superimposition, that the shadow cast by the sun in that picture is not at odds with the superimposed sun.

**Superimposing these 2 shots
gives this result**

90 Is there a special technique for photographing fireworks or lightning?

■ ■

The technique is identical in both cases.

You can use either daylight colour film or else types A or B for artificial light. The latter are preferable if you want a slightly hot colour rendering.

There are two ways to proceed:

a) Hand hold the camera and shoot at between 1/30 and 1/100 sec., with the aperture at f/4 or f/5.6, for 40 ASA emulsions;

b) I prefer to use a tripod and short exposure (on "B", at infinity), in order to get several firework patterns on the same negative.

I do not like to shoot fireworks by itself. It is better to include a monument, a building or just some trees in the foreground, in order to give some proportion and interest to the shot.

Lightning should obviously be photographed from indoors, away from the rain. Mount your camera on a tripod and set up by a window which faces most of the lightning. Follow the same procedures as for fireworks.

Here is a table for approximate exposure times:

Shutter open at "B" or "T"

Subject	25 - 40 ASA	64 - 80 ASA	125 - 160 - 400 ASA
Fireworks	f/5.6 - f/8	f/8 - f/11	f/11 - f/16 - f/22
Lightning	f/4 - f/5.6	f/5.6 - f/8	f/8 - f/11 - f/16

Fireworks shot with electronic flash.

The shutter remained open for about 2 min., long enough to record 2 flashes.

With the camera on a tripod and the aperture at f/8 (Tri-X), the flash lights up the statue in the foreground.

With the aperture at f/8 using Tri-X film, 5 or 6 bursts of fireworks are recorded. If you look closely, you will see as treetlamp in the photo as well.

91

Why do the subjects I have photographed with flash often have red eyes?

■■■■■■■■■■■■■■■■■■■■■■■■■

This annoying problem is as common as it is easy to solve.

It is invariably the result of shooting with the flash very close to the axis of the lens (flash attached to the camera).

The problem results when the subject (person, animal, etc.) is in a poorly lit room. The strong light given off by the flash is so rapid that the iris of the eye does not have time to close.

In this situation, the subject is looking at the camera.

As a result, the light from the flash is reflected off the membrane behind the retina of the eye and produces a red or amber tint in colour photos and a white spot in black and white photos.

There are several solutions: a) light the room as much as possible and ask the subject to stare at a light source for a moment just before shooting; b) keep the flash two or three feet from the camera; c) make the subject look away from the camera.

This is what happens if flash is used in the dark and it is held too close to the lens.

92 How can I average the exposure time for a full moon with the longer exposure time required for a moonlit landscape?

It is practically impossible to average them out since the light margin between the two is so great.

A full moon by itself requires an average exposure of about 1/125 sec. at f/5.6 or f/8, with a daylight or type-B colour film of 100 to 125 ASA.

Remember that the moon derives its light from the sun: in other words, it reflects "daylight". But to photograph a moonlit landscape — even with a full moon and cloudless sky — the exposure time mentioned above is far too short.

To achieve a perfect exposure for this kind of landscape, you must run several exposure tests at 30 sec., 1 minute, 3 minutes, etc. The ideal aperture is f/5.6. If you keep the moon in the shot, such a long exposure will wash it out; it will look like a shooting star, because it will have moved several degrees.

Assuming you have a camera equipped to do double exposures, the trick is to make a superimposition, with two exposure times. (See Question 89)

First, shoot the moonlit landscape with a regular lens for one to two minutes, with the moon itself out of frame. You will have to decide beforehand where the moon is going to be situated once you have taken the second shot. Remember also to keep roughly the top third of the frame clear of trees, buildings and other objects which might silhouette themselves against the horizon.

Take off the regular lens and replace it with a 135mm or even a 300mm. This will allow you to locate the moon at the precise spot you intend as well as to give the moon a more imposing size. The second exposure has to be very short, about 1/250 sec. at f/4 for type-B or daylight colour film.

For readers who might not be aware of it, a professional photographer often get excellent moonlit shots in full daylight, with a single exposure. Most night scenes in feature films are shot this way. Use a film for artificial light, without any correction filter, then simply underexpose it two or three stops. The results are striking: a very blue cast and a loss of detail in foreground objects, which really gives an effect of moonlight.

The same method applies for black and white except that you use a very dark red filter and underexpose two stops.

These two methods are the only ones which will allow you to shoot a moonlit scene with one exposure. You should also use a lens that is a little longer than normal. This will give the moon proportions which more closely resemble what we are used to seeing.

If you want to keep the sun in your photo and create a similar effect, wait until the sun disappears behind a cloud. Any strong light or shadow created by it is thereby eliminated. This will give your photo more realism.

Midnight. Lighting: 2 street-lamps. Tri-X, 800 ASA — 5 sec. at f/5.6.

Same conditions but exposed 20 sec. at f/5.6.

Same conditions but exposed 3 minutes at f/5.6. Another 3 minutes and it would have been impossible to print the shot, because the negative would have been too dense. Even at midnight an overexposure is possible.

93

After developing a film, I was surprised to notice that it was filled with what seemed to be "electric" flashes. What could have caused this?

∎∎∎∎∎∎∎∎∎∎∎∎∎∎∎∎∎∎∎∎∎∎∎∎∎∎∎∎∎

Your problem is very simple, as well as quite common. Like many beginners (and professionals) you probably rewound your film **too quickly.**

Always be careful in your handling of the camera; this rule applies particularly to how you release the shutter (you may get a blurring if you do it too abruptly), and to the way you lay the camera down on a table. Remember that you are handling a very delicate tool, moreover, it is loaded with film that is just as delicate.

"Electric flashes" generally occur when it is cold or humid. Some forgetful photographers load or rewind their film too quickly, and thereby produce **static electricity** where the emulsion touches the back of the film.

To rationalize his error, a photographer will tell you that the effect was produced deliberately to make the photo more "artistic" — sometimes this works!

To suggest a remedy seems pointless: one usually does not consider the cold or humidity factor when shooting. There is not much you can do except to load and rewind slowly. To rub antistatic agent on those parts of the camera which come in contact with the film is a waste of time.

These flashes of static electricity are, appropriately enough, over the head of rock singer Robert Charlebois.

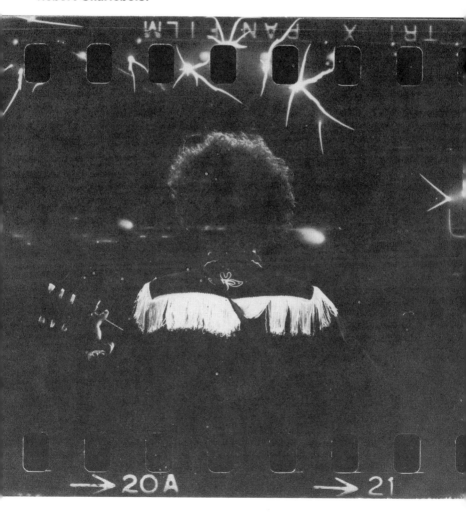

94 How can I do double exposures with any kind of 35mm camera?

With a few exceptions, it is easy to do double exposures with any modern 35mm.

One technique applies to most makes of camera, with the notable exception of the Nikon.

Release the shutter and take your first photo; press the rewind button and hold it down while you cock the shutter again. The film cannot move because the button disengages the sprockets that advance the film.

The Pentax H-A and H3V, the Spotmatic, the Nikkormat and several others work like this. You can be certain the film will not move. You can repeat the operation two, three or even four times if you wish.

For those who own a Nikon, there is a 5-step procedure:

a) take the first picture;

b) the ring which sits around the shutter-release has to be turned to the right (as though you were rewinding), such that the white dot on the ring faces the letter "R";

c) take note of the position of the small red dot on the shutter-release and turn the rewind arm (on top of the camera, to the left) clockwise until the small red dot has made a complete circle;

d) turn the ring which sits around the shutter-release to the left, to the letter "A";

e) cock the shutter until it won't move any more. You are now ready for the second exposure and confident that the film is in exactly the same place as it was for the first shot.

For other makes of camera, consult their instruction booklets.

The first shot was made with a yellow filter (and the cooperation of the subject), underexposing 1 stop. The second (to get the sun only) was made with a ND filter and a 25A red filter. This is the result, after 4 attempts...

95

How can I get good contrast and clarity when copying an old brown or sepia daguerreotype or other old photo?

■ I

It will help to equip your lens with a dark blue filter, such as the No. 47 (or C5), and use panchromatic film.

If you are working very close to the subject and your camera will take other lenses, it is better to add a bellows than a close-up lens. In this way you will only have to add a filter to the lens.

You can achieve a significant increase in contrast by using the proven method of underexposing a little and developing slightly longer.

Use a more contrasty developer such as D-19, and print on a more contrasty paper (No. 4 or No. 5).

As illustrated in the pictures on these two pages, you can copy the photos you get in department-store photo machines even if they have become really dog-eared after years at the bottom of a purse. It is not easy for a beginner, but the best method is to copy onto 4 x 5 Ektapan (Kodak) and then very carefully retouch the copy. You can see the amazing results that are possible on the opposite page. You will notice that the copy reveals marks which are not even visible on the original. This process works for all old photographs.

The original photo, measuring 2 x 2½ inches.

Copy on 4 x 5 film.

Retouched copy.

96 How can I get a very dark sky with colour or black and white film?

∎∎∎∎∎∎∎∎∎∎∎∎∎∎∎∎∎∎∎∎∎∎∎∎∎∎∎∎∎∎∎

First of all, the sky should be clear without a cloud from one horizon to the other.

A blue sky is darkened when the blue radiations are absorbed by a yellow, orange or red contrast filter, depending on how much darkening is desired. A pale yellow filter will darken the sky less than a red filter because the red has much greater power to absorb blue.

Large white clouds, which are unaffected by the filter, become more pronounced and stand out against a dark sky.

To guarantee a black sky use infrared film with a red filter.

In colour photography, there is only one way to get a dark sky: Use a polarizing filter. If placed at the **recommended angle** (see instructions accompanying it) the filter not only darkens the sky, but also produces greater colour saturation.

As a last reminder, don't forget to take the exposure coefficient of these filters into account.

Tri-X, 650 ASA, without filter.

Tri-X, 650 ASA, with red No. 25 filter.

High Infrared film. Not recommended for shooting people.

97 How can I photograph the same person several times on the same negative?

∎ ∎

This is a technique that everyone should know. To make it work, you must use a black background. The background can be a piece of black material or a black wall, but it is important that it not be lit either directly or from the side. The slightest irregularity will be certain to show up in the photograph. Mount the camera on a tripod and be sure that the camera's field of view is free of any lighted object.

Now, introduce a person into the frame, and be careful to place him well to the right or left. It is helpful to imagine a line running down the centre of the frame that your subject cannot cross, or otherwise there will be a risk of overlapping images.

Lighting the subject is very important. If he is close to the wall, you will have to light from the side. If he is at least 10 feet away, side lighting is unnecessary.

Take the first shot. Try to capture a variety of expressions so that the different images of your subject will contrast with one another. Assuming your camera is equipped for double exposures, you simply cock it again and proceed with the second shot. Make sure the subject now appears in the half of the frame left empty during the first shot. Since the background is black, no image will appear in this half of the frame. You can now photograph the same person many times on the same negative.

You can accomplish much the same thing outdoors during the evening, by using "open flash". This makes the task much easier. With the shutter open, the subject can move in front of the camera without being registered on the film. The subject's different poses are caught by the manual firing of the flash.

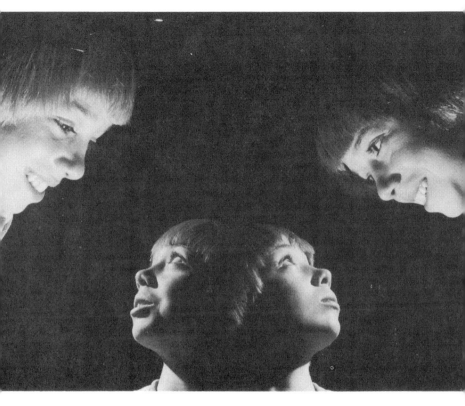

As described in the text...

98 Is it necessary for amateurs to use a tripod for speeds of 1/30 sec. or slower?

This is only a suggestion, not a hard-and-fast rule, and it is therefore open to debate. The end results will be purely a function of how steady the hands are that hold the camera. It is not entirely surprising to hear that some professional may have shot a photo at ⅛ or even ½ sec., hand-held, without a tripod. There are a number of tricks that the photographer should know about holding his camera. If he has learned to hold it on end, when necessary, so that his forehead is in contact with the maximum possible surface area of the camera back; if he has learned to spread his legs about 2 feet, one foot just ahead of the other; if he has learned to press his elbows against his sides to make them act like two feet of a tripod, while his head and neck act like the other foot, then this photographer can afford to leave his tripod at home. (See Question 80)

Certain kinds of photographic work, by their very nature, demand a maximum of efficiency and mobility, and therefore a minimum of equipment. Under these conditions a tripod becomes cumbersome and unwanted. It is difficult to conceal a camera that has a tripod attached and it is usually not too difficult to find some support on the spot. When the light is so poor that you are forced to expose at ¼, ½, 1 sec., use a lamp-post, park bench, table, fire hydrant, wall, fence post or even your car window (with the motor off).

I should point out here that coupled rangefinder cameras, especially the Leica, are incredibly stable. The shutter-release on the Leica is very light and vibration-free, while SLR's tend to vibrate with the motion of the mirror. Moreover, the blackout encountered with an open shutter causes you to lose contact with the subject. For certain special shooting conditions, such as during the evening and particularly with colour, the coupled rangefinder camera really has many more advantages.

The right elbow is held firmly against the ribs, the left hand presses the camera against the forehead.

The camera can be steadied by pulling against the strap, which is around the neck. This is recommended for shooting wide-angle shots without looking through the viewfinder, even at slow shutter speeds.

Steady the camera by holding it against the ground.

By putting your fingers between the ground and the camera, and pressing firmly, you can shoot as slow as $1/2$ sec.

99

What equipment do I need to set up a small "professional" studio, and how much might it cost?

■ I

To work comfortably in a studio, you need a minimum 12 x 16 foot space.

You will have to install a mounting for the rolls of paper which serve as a backdrop.

Obtain one roll in black and another in white. These can be unrolled from ceiling to floor to cover all the space in front of the camera. The paper forms a continuous background and leaves no trace of the floor.

If you want to set up a reasonably professional studio, you will have to be prepared to spend some money since the equipment is fairly expensive.

Professionals rarely work with direct light. Instead they use white umbrellas in conjunction with electronic flash.

A 4 x 5 camera is not an absolute necessity, but proves to be extremely useful (about $300).

Electronic flash units should have three heads and a 400 to 800 W booster. Prices vary, but you should count on a minimum of $400.

Add to that the price of a good solid tripod, three umbrellas, a studio bench, photoflood or quartz lamps (depending on needs), two large translucent reflectors, and so on. A minimum of $1,500 would be a conservative estimate.

Of course, you can operate on a smaller scale by using your present cameras (35mm or 2¼ x 2¼), and by buying a smaller flash unit, or simply sticking with photofloods. It is wise to start off slowly; acquire extra equipment when it is needed and when you can afford it.

Basic equipment for a small studio — 2 lamps and a backdrop.

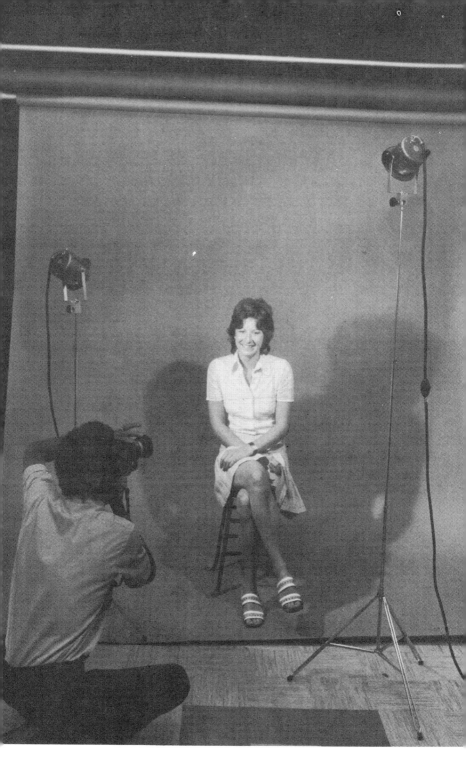

100 Is there any way to improve my efforts as a portrait photographer while using a general purpose 35mm lens?

All lenses of a focal length less than 50mm are considered wide-angle. As their angle of view increases — 35mm, 28mm, 24mm, 21mm — there is marked distortion of a subject shot in close-up. Apart from special effects (for example, fashion photos in which the proportions of the model are exaggerated), the use of wide-angles for for portraits and general photography should not be considered.

No one will deny the usefulness of the wide-angles for shooting panoramically, especially when the photographer is not able to distance himself for a long shot. This is why wide-angle lenses are available. But you must be careful to avoid shooting subjects from too close or using shooting angles which are too severe. Otherwise, your subject will be distorted beyond recognition.

I realize that those of you who have cameras with a fixed lens have little choice. These cameras usually make close-up portraits impossible since few can be focussed at less than three to four feet. Thus, a ¾ shot becomes necessary. If the lens is of good quality, you can easily overcome the problem by enlarging a specific section of the negative.

As a final suggestion, you might try transforming your 35mm lens into a 105mm lens with the aid of a "focal tripler". The slight loss of definition caused by a tripler makes it perfect for portraits; sharpness is often undesirable in portraits (especially in the case of people of a certain age).

24 mm lens. The angle is too low for this type of photo.

24 mm lens. In my opinion, the angle is too high.

135 mm lens. No distortion, even at low angles.

101 What is the ideal combination of lenses for covering all subjects and situations?

■ ■

The professionals are not in total agreement about this combination. There are several possibilities:

1st choice – 21mm 35mm 90mm
2nd choice – 28mm 50mm 105mm
3rd choice – 35mm 85mm 135mm

My own choice would not be anyone of these, but a combination of the 1st and 3rd: 21mm, 85mm, 135mm.

The reason is very simple. Press work usually involves the photographer in one of two extreme situations: either he has to work very close to his subject or else very far away. That is why few press photographers use a standard (50mm) lens.

More often than not, a photographer works indoors, in cramped quarters where his only choice of lens can be a 21mm or 24mm wide-angle. On the other hand, if it is necessary to keep a low profile and to work at some distance away for reasons of discretion or safety, he will choose between 2 lenses: the junior telephoto (85mm) or the 135mm telephoto. Both are ideal for outdoor photography because they allow you to keep your distance from the subject — therefore allowing the subject to remain more relaxed.

Finally, I do not want to leave an impression that I have anything against the standard lens. On the contrary, let us recall that the great master Henri-Cartier Bresson rarely uses anything but a standard lens.

35 mm Nikkor

58 mm Nikkor

105 mm Nikkor

105 mm + doubler = 210 mm

500 mm Catadioptric

500 mm catadioptric + doubler = 1,000 mm

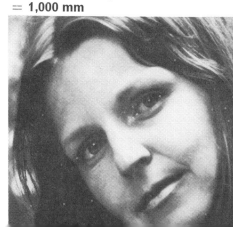

102 Can I create grain deliberately in my colour photos, as is done so often now with black and white?

■ ■

The procedure for colour photos is the same as for black and white. All you need to do is ignore the rated speed of the film and use it at 250 or even 500 ASA, instead of the usual 64 or 80 ASA.

The developing time of your boosted film should be increased by 75% in the first developer. Any boosted film must be over-developed: this is what gives it the high degree of grain and contrast.

You can get even more grain at the printing stage by blowing up just one part of the negative.

Remember, this process will upset the colour rendering, and create a colour cast which you may not find desirable. But this seems to be the price you must pay for artistic experimentation...

Almost all backlit shots will result in a lot of grain. The photo on the opposite page has been shot with a special screen designed to create a grainy effect with both colour and black and white film.

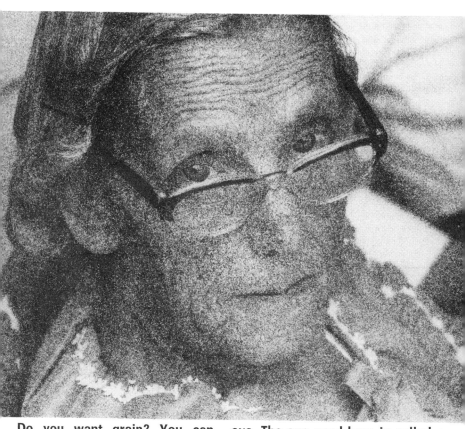

Do you want grain? You can place a screen directly on the photo and press it into place with glass. This film, which comes in plastic sheets, contains very fine grains which are almost invisible to the naked eye. The one used here is called "mezzotinto". There are some 20 other textures to choose from. Write Mortensen Photographic, 7557 Sunset Blvd., Hollywood, Cal. 90046.

103 How can I most effectively photograph a nude?

Of all the different kinds of abstract art, I think the nude has the most popular following in photography. Most serious photographers have at one time or another attempted nude photography in styles which include the abstract, romantic, unreal surreal, stylised, or for a daring few, blatantly pornographic. For me, the nude offers the widest range of possibilities for artistic expressiveness. There is no greater challange to a photographer's creativity than the beauty of the female body.

A searching eye will discover a universe of shapes, lines, contours and textures; the photographer is limited only by his own sensitivity to the subject matter. The beginner should attempt his first experiments against a black backdrop. Since it is no secret that shadow plays an important role in this kind of photography, frontal lighting should be avoided. A single light source will highlight certain shapes and obscure others.

The essence of nude photography is to accentuate lines by side or even back-lighting. Diffuse lighting is also recommended. This is the time to use contrasty photo techniques, but without giving the impression that they have been executed on Kodalith. In a word, the nude should express simplicity. The best examples keep tonalities to a minimum and are the result of a carefully chosen shooting angle. Except in special cases, avoid using a wide-angle lens. The best professional results are achieved with a standard lens, or even an 85 or 105mm.

Photo by Arthur Gladu.

The erotic flower pot.

104 What camera provides the best value for underwater photography?

■■■■■■■■■■■■■■■■■■■■■■■■■■■■

In my opinion, the camera which stands up best under adverse conditions is the Nikonos 35mm. It is designed to withstand water to a depth of 150 feet and will withstand just about everything else: sand, snow, salt water, dust and above all, cold. You can even scrub it inside and out.

The Nikonos has no range-finder (you couldn't use one anyway), and it is sold with a choice of 3 lenses: 35mm, 28mm, and fisheye. I prefer a 28mm lens which offers a much greater field of view than the 35mm. The 28mm is best under water because the phenomenon of refraction makes objects appear larger, and makes them seem only about ¾ of their actual distance away. You could infer from this that under water a 35mm equals a 50mm, a 28mm, a 35mm, etc. The reason for this, of course, is the difference between the indices of refraction in air and water.

Many special techniques are required for underwater photography. The rate of light diffusion and absorption is such that the light level decreases sharply with the depth of the water. Therefore, use of a fast black and white film (400 ASA) is advised.

Underwater, light quickly becomes monochromatic. Radiations in the visible spectrum are filtered and absorbed according to the density of the water. Radiations of a longer wave-length, such as red, start falling off at around 10 to 15 feet, orange, yellow, green and blue below that. As a result, blue is the dominant cast in slides taken under water without flash.

As a final, perhaps needless, reminder: all your equipment, flash, light meter, etc., can only be used under water if it is perfectly sealed, otherwise it may suffer permanent damage.

Three enthusiastic divers getting ready to go down with camera equipment and all.

A diver at work under the ice.

Photo by
J.C. Paquet

105 How can I develop the confidence and dexterity of a professional photographer?

∎ ∎

The behaviour of some photographers is calculatedly off-handed, and verges on sheer abandon. However, it is undeniable that it takes time to reach this degree of competence.

The professional photographer must know his equipment inside and out. If, for example, he is working with a wide-angle, he will always have it set on the hyperfocal. (See Question 130) That means no focussing for any subject from seven feet to infinity. Also there is no need to keep the camera at eye level. He knows that a wide-angle covers a field of about 80° in the horizontal plane and 60° in the vertical. Experience has taught him that by holding the camera perpendicular, with the axis of the lens right in line with the subject, his framing will be fairly reliable.

Professional photographers learn to shoot while on the move, by using the fastest shutter speed (1/1000 sec.) and slowing down only momentarily for the shot. They know by experience to turn the aperture ring to the right or left for open or closed, **without looking.** They may, for example, be already open to f/2.8 and adjust by turning to the left and counting the number of clicks as they pass f/4, f/5.6, etc. This is the kind of gesture that becomes second nature to the professional photographer. Have you ever tried to focus on a child playing on a seesaw? Do you think you could focus on someone as they fell off a bridge? The secret is to be able to shoot immediately, to be **ready** at all times.

As you can see, there really is **no** secret. It is all technique, skill, experience and an ability to anticipate the unexpected.

Len Sideway, of "The Gazette", shooting a certain gentleman at the microphone.

No picture taking please! . . . No, sister... (click).

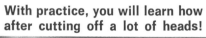

With practice, you will learn how after cutting off a lot of heads!

106 What can I do when there is not enough room between the lights and the subject in a close-up shot?

I am tempted to recommend simply a Circo flash, and all your problems would be solved. This type of flash surrounds the lens.

It is difficult when the lighting falls on either side of the camera at 45°; lateral lighting creates unpleasant shadows (see Question 83 on distant close-up shots). If you must be close to the subject you will have to light it indirectly with reflectors placed at different angles.

You might be surprised to learn that for extreme close-ups the best thing is actually backlight, **directed towards the subject** by reflectors (fill light).

It is interesting, for example, to see the effects of backlight on flowers and leaves. The sun diffuses them with a very warm light and makes them semi-transparent. Many flower photographers use a 10 x 12 in. piece of cardboard covered with a piece of crumpled aluminum foil as their reflector. It is then a simple matter of cutting a hole in the centre big enough for a reflex lens. It is inexpensive and efficient, especially if you take the trouble to curve the reflector a little.

Another method is to make a four-panel reflector out of white cardboard. The four panels partially surround the subject and reflect a very diffuse, shadow-free light.

The circular flash (in the shape of a doughnut) mentioned above is designed to wrap around the lens and is also shadow-free. Its special construction allows you to light places which are otherwise inaccessible, such as the inside of the mouth.

Photo with backlight and without fill light.

...and fit it over a piece of cardboard that has a hole for the lens.

Just crumple a piece of aluminum foil...

107 In still photography, how is a "blur" most effectively created?

Every professional photographer has deliberately created blur at some time or other. Still photography does not have the added dimension of movement that the cinema enjoys. The photographer is restricted to shooting one photograph at a time, whether this be every 2 seconds or every 10 seconds. His finished product is always "frozen" while in the cinema it is possible to shoot 16 to 128 images per second and thereby allow movement to be reproduced on a screen.

Nevertheless, it is still possible in photography to create an impression of movement by "freezing" the subject in the right way. This is where the shutter becomes important. By shooting at a speed of 1/1000 sec., you obviously never get a blur, deliberate or otherwise. At this shutter speed you stop all ordinary movement, independent of the angle of movement in relation to the camera. Even at 1/60 sec., you can stop a subject running toward the camera. As a rule, you should increase the shutter speed proportionately as the subject's angle of displacement tends towards the perpendicular.

Several other factors must be considered to get the right shutter speed: the distance from the subject, the speed at which the subject is travelling, the focal length of the lens, and the angle of displacement in relation to the axis of the camera. If you take all these carefully into account, your pictures will be clear and sharp. But the fun really begins for the photo buff when he chooses to ignore the rules and shoot like a film-maker. In other words, he follows the subject as it moves, shooting it at a fairly low shutter speed (1/60 or 1/125 sec.), and keeps with it until it has stopped.

The success rate for this kind of photograph depends on the individual photographer's skill (I get about one good photo in every three). In the following illustrations, you will see a shot in which the subject is sharp, whereas the background is out of focus or blurred. It really gives an impression of motion. The opposite effect can be achieved by using a slower shutter speed; the subject can then be "blurred" against a fairly sharp, distant background. At the slower shutter speeds, the photographer will have to use a neutral density filter, otherwise a fast emulsion will be badly overexposed.

Following the subject, as if with a movie camera. Tri-X — 1/125 sec. at f/16, with a ND 2X filter — 800 ASA.

A fast exposure freezes the subject. Tri-X — 1/500 sec. at f/16, — 800 ASA.

108 How do I photograph a TV screen and get a clear picture, in both colour and black and white?

■ I

With 35mm, a tripod must be used to photograph any black and white TV. You will discover that it is impossible to shoot a screen with a focal plane shutter at speeds higher than 1/15 sec. Because this shutter moves from left to right and a TV screen is swept or scanned from top to bottom, a dark diagonal line will appear on the film.

You will, therefore, have to refrain from shooting subjects in motion.

Make the focussing easier by centring on the frame around the screen.

Adjust the TV image for optimum contrast and darken any windows to eliminate the possibility of reflections.

Using a tripod, place the camera in a central position a few inches from the screen, and make any adjustment in the distance to get the right vertical and horizontal framing.

Never use flash directly on the screen because it will make the image disappear.

A colour TV image is formed differently from a black and white one. There is no need to use a slow shutter speed; with colour, any speed is possible.

Daylight colour film always gives the best results.

You can, without affecting the quality of the image, use indirect flash (on the ceiling) in order to provide some general room lighting and make the set visible. **This does not affect the exposure time.**

Those who have through-the-lens metering can get a perfect reading from the screen with their meter.

The right exposure — for colour — is generally around 1/60 sec. at f/2.8 or f/4 with 160 ASA film, depending on the brightness of the picture.

No light in the room. Exposure for the screen (colour) only. Tri-X, 1/125 sec. at f/5.6 — 800 ASA, or daylight colour, 1/160. at f/3.5 — 160 ASA.

Tri-X, 1/60, sec. at f/8 — 800 ASA, with bounced flash.

Here's what happens when you use flash to photograph a TV screen.

Focal plane shutter, 35 mm, Tri-X, 1/15 sec. at f/11 — 800 ASA.

Focal plane shutter, 35 mm, Tri-X, 1/60 sec. at f/5.6 — 800 ASA.

109 If shooting indoors with well balanced lighting, is it necessary to change the aperture when I move my camera forwards or backwards?

Not at all. What counts here is the distance between the lamps and the subject. You shoot at a particular aperture because of the intensity of the light reflected by the subject. You will therefore have to open or close the diaphragm when **the lamps** are moved in relation to the subject. This will increase or decrease the intensity of the reflected light. You are free to move your camera back and forth over a distance of several feet without having to change the aperture.

The diaphragm opening or closing is determined according to the law of the "inverted square", which says that the intensity of the light varies inversely with the square of the distance. For example: a 100 W bulb lighting a surface 1 foot away has an intensity "x". When this same surface is 2 feet away, it will only receive light equal in intensity to a 25 W bulb.

This principle can be easily verified using a light meter, or else use a tape measure to check the distances involved. It is easy to see that if a subject is 6 feet from a 1000 W lamp, and you double the distance (12 feet) it will receive only 250 W. You must, therefore, open up two stops.

Moving the camera backward and forward does not affect the exposure. But moving the lamps backward or forward affects the exposure according to the law of the inverted square.

Subject

Camera

Lamp

110

I understand that you photographed the birth of your little girl. Hospitals are very strict about their rules and they say that the delivery-room door is not opened for anyone. What preparations did you make?

∎ ∎

Perhaps every photographer's greatest desire is to take his child's first picture. Moved by a sense of paternal pride, he can hardly wait for an excuse to take a little photo from his wallet and say: "That's him! And I took the picture!

I did indeed photograph my daughter's birth seven or eight years ago. Here is how it happened. First of all, I had to get permission from three sources: from the director of the hospital, the head of the obstetrics department in the hospital and from my family doctor. As far as the doctor was concerned, there was no problem; he was perfectly willing. The director of the hospital hesitated two months before saying that "if it's all right with the head of the department, its all right with me ..." I finally managed to persuade the department head by telling her that I was doing an article for a well-known magazine (it was only published a year later in fact). She did impose one restriction: I would only be admitted to the delivery room if the

birth took place during the evening ... But my doctor said, "Don't worry. Whether it's day or night, you'll get in." Dressed like a doctor, with mask, green jacket and all the equipment for shooting both colour and black and white, I walked into the delivery room and ... it all went well.

I think the restrictions are less severe today.

"If you have the right intentions and know your family doctor well," says my new family doctor, "you should have no trouble." The only problem is that most husbands do not have the stamina for such an event, and the doctor is likely to find himself having to look after both husband and wife!

The atmosphere in a delivery room can become very tense. The photographer must therefore know what he is doing and keep out of the way so he does not disturb anything. There is no need to think of extra lighting: what is already there is ample. With a Tri-X film of 1600 ASA, you can easily shoot hand-held at 1/125 sec. and f/4. For type-B colour, 1/30 sec. at f/2.8 will do it. The presence of "spots" in certain places may alter these exposures. Through-the-lens metering is therefore a must. Remember, you must be well prepared in advance, because the birth itself only lasts about 30 seconds. Congratulations to the new father!

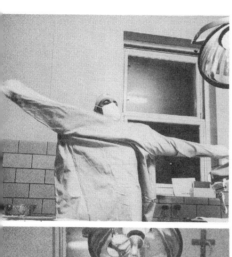

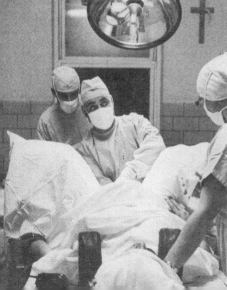

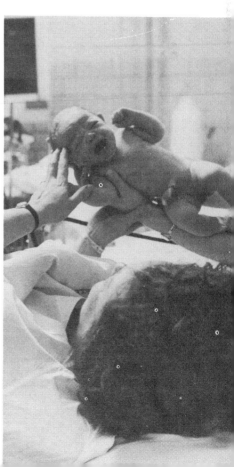

111

How do you create a relaxed atmosphere when shooting?

■ ■

My job is never to create an atmosphere when I shoot, but rather, to record whatever the mood happens to be at that moment. It is as simple as that! If my presence as a photographer is apt to make people nervous, you can be sure that I will do everything possible to make myself inconspicuous, at least for long enough to take my pictures. If necessary I will even refrain from lifting my camera to eye level. Believe me, shooting without "aiming" is not unusual. (See Question 105)

It is amazing how much more relaxed people are when they are being themselves. Obviously, the presence of a photographer does not put most people at their ease, and many will react by averting their glance or turning their back. But with much skill, speed and patience, a good photographer will succeed in catching people off guard, when they are behaving naturally. Moreover, there will always be people who will bend over backwards to get themselves included in the picture. Remember, the photographer is in some sense a mirror of society; let us be content with an honest reflection of the way things are and leave elaborate set-ups to actors and art photographers.

It's amazing how natural people can be when they don't notice the photographer...

First of all, thousands of good photographs are taken every day by photographers who have no expertise in this field. Yet it is also true that an understanding of the photographic process, with the opportunity this affords of really controlling results, is incomplete without some understanding of the rudiments of sensitometry.

Density refers to the degree which a particular portion of a negative or print has darkened. While a negative is evaluated by the amount of light that passes through it (transmission), a print is read by reflected light (reflection). In both cases, density is a measure of the amount of light transmitted or reflected. For example, that part of a negative that transmits 50% of the incident light has a density of 0.30. The table below gives a number of equivalencies.

Here are a few average density values to serve as references for the reader:

white on a paper proof	1.05
black on a matte paper proof	1.40
black on a glossy paper proof	1.70
Transparent area on a heavily exposed negative	0.20
opaque area on a negative with normal contrast	1.30
opaque area on a negative with low contrast	0.90
opaque area on a negative with high contrast	1.60

% of light trans- mitted or reflected	Corresponding Density	% of light trans- mitted or reflected	Corresponding Density
100%	0.00	5%	1.30
80%	0.10	4%	1.40
64%	0.20	2%	1.70
50%	.30	1%	2.00
20%	.70		
10%	1.00		

In rating a negative, the most important factor is the **density** range: the difference between the highest and lowest densities, or in other words, the brightest highlights and darkest shadows in the photograph. This range is generally taken to indicate the **contrast** of the negative.

A negative is said to be **standard** in terms of contrast when it can be printed satisfactorily on a No. 2 paper without need for modifications. The density range of a standard negative is about 1.10. Notice that the type of enlarger being used affects the choice of paper for printing: thus a negative which gives good results on a No. 2 paper with a condenser-type enlarger will have to be printed on a hard No. 3 paper with a diffusion-type enlarger.

A negative is said to be **soft** or **extra-soft** if it must be printed on a No. 3, 4 or 5 paper. Its density range may be as low as 0.60. On the other hand, a negative is considered **hard** or **extra-hard** when it must be printed on No. 1 or No. 0 paper. In this case, the density will be about 1.50.

(Photo by R.W.)

113 What is the characteristic curve of an emulsion?

This term is often found in technical photographic literature and most serious photographers run across it in their reading sooner or later. Moreover, the concept of **characteristic curve** is part of sensitometry, and an understanding of it is useful to both the professional and the novice.

In a developed negative, the degree of blackening or density varies with the quantity of light it received at the time of exposure: for example, a white wall is "lighter" than a red-brick wall. Every object in a scene is reproduced on the negative by an image of a given density. If you were to re-arrange the picture so that the objects were all put in order from darkest to lightest, their negative images would be in order of increasing density. By measuring the quantity of light reflected by the various objects (the luminous energy), and their corresponding densities on the negative, one can draw a graph of the variations in density compared to the variations in luminous energy.

This graph gives us an idea of what a real characteristic curve is like. It is made in a laboratory, where, instead of exposing the film to only a selective range of luminous energy, it is exposed to a very wide range. The technicians can now draw a thorough characteristic curve, one which is a real **portrait** of the emulsion being studied.

The first thing to notice is that the density readings obtained will generally fall into a straight rising line. The density range of the negative may be calculated by subtracting the lowest density reading from the highest. You can see how the contrast of the negative, measured by its density range, is related to the slope of the characteristic curve: the steeper the surve, the higher the contrast, and vice versa. Also keep in mind the importance of several developing parameters (type of developer, length of development, temperature, etc.) to the slope of the curve and therefore to the **final contrast** of the negative.

Two other very important points will help us to understand certain exposure errors. At the left end of the curve note that the film will not react to luminous energy below a certain quantity "A" (which is different for each type of emulsion). There is **no density** to be measured and no image is recorded: this is what happens when a negative is underexposed.

At the other end of the curve we have a different but similar problem. The **maximum possible density** is reached when the illuminations rise to a certain level "D", beyond which the emulsion cannot record details of the objects in question. Thus overexposure causes a loss of detail.

AB: Heel
BC: Rectilinear portion
CD: Shoulder

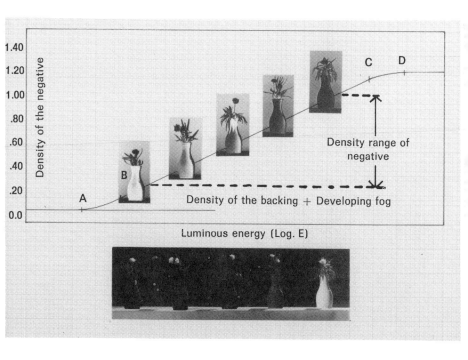

114

I shot some portraits around noon on a sunny summer day. Even though I paid careful attention to my meter readings, why were the shadows completely underexposed?

For any scene being photographed there are two factors to take into consideration:

a) Every object possesses a certain light reflecting power which makes it light or dark;

b) the lighting almost always consists of **direct light** (the sun, for example) which creates shadows, and secondary sources made up of **reflected light,** which comes from surfaces like a ceiling, walls, sand, etc. (even a newspaper can act as a good reflector for portrait purposes). It is only this reflected light that will fall on those areas of the subject known as **shadows.** Those areas which are lit directly and most brightly are called **highlights.**

Let us take an example and see how it applies to portraiture. The subject is lit from the side by a main light with an intensity of 1000 units of luminous energy (an arbitrary measure). The shadowy side is illuminated by reflected light of 250 units. Under these conditions, with human skin (Caucasian) reflecting about 35% of the light, the side of the face reflects 35% x 1000 = 350 units, while the shadowy side reflects only 35%

x 250 = 87 units. The same formula can be applied to other parts of the subject according to the table opposite.

We have now discovered the concept of the **brightness range,** which has a lot to do with many an under-or overexposed negative. This brightness factor is the **ratio** between the minimum and maximum quantities of reflected light. In the accompanying chart, white fur reflects the maximum (750 units), and dark fabric the minimum (12 units). The ratio 12:750 = 1:63 is the brightness range for this particular subject. To put it another way, this represents the number of different values contained by this subject (63) and which **must be recorded on the negative by different densities.**

After this long detour, we can now return to the original question and see that the problem is an over-extended brightness range, accompanied by an exposure calculated on the basis of the highlights and not the shadows. On a sunny summer day, the light creates shadows that are hard and insufficiently opened by ambient light. The subject's high number of light values greatly exceeds the capacities of the emulsion (especially with colour). The underexposure of the shadows is therefore not the fault of the light meter.

What is the solution? Avoid shooting portraits at noon; instead choose a time of day when the sun is low or obscured. Reduce the brightness range by using a reflector or a small flash. Shade or backlight the subject. Expose for the shadows and reduce developing time by about 25%.

Units of Reflected Light

% of reflectance		Bright portion (1000 units)	Dark portion (250 units)
White fur	75%	750	187
Skin	35%	350	87
Hair	10%	100	25
Dark fabric	5%	50	12

(Continued overleaf)

(Photo by R.W.)

115 Is there a relationship between the brightness range of the subject and the characteristic curve of the emulsion?

■ ■

Two points follow from the preceeding discussion:

a) Each particular scene has a certain number of light values (determined by the brightness range) which must be recorded on the film in different densities.

b) The number of light values that an emulsion can record is limited by its minimum and maximum density (points A and D on the characteristic curve). If the light signal is too weak, there is underexposure and loss of detail. If it is too strong, there is again a loss of detail, this time because of overexposure.

In order to avoid bad reproduction, the extreme densities on the curve — the **shoulder** (CD) portion and the **heel** (AB) portion — are not normally used. The normal exposure area is the **rectilinear** (BC) portion.

There is, therefore, a **brightness** range for the emulsion itself which we have in effect defined. To obtain a correct exposure (the right combination of aperture and shutter speed) make sure that the subject's **main values** (its brightness range) fall **within** the brightness range of the emulsion. The exposure is then said to fall within the rectilinear portion of the curve. The

light meter is calibrated for taking this into account in average shooting situations.

Modern emulsions offer a fairly wide brightness range, something in the order of 1:250. But if you attempt to photograph a scene with a wider brightness range, and follow the manufacturer's recommendations on developing, the resulting negative will have far too much contrast to be reproduced without losses.

In practical terms, the optimum brightness range, given a standard developing time, is roughly 1:64. This corresponds to a maximum spread of 6 stops between the light value extremes of the subject being photographed. (See Question 116) The correct exposure would allow all values in the scene to be recorded on the rectilinear part of the characteristic curve, and standard development would assure a proper range of densities.

As the brightness range increases, there is an encroachment on the extreme ends of the characteristic curve. This can be partially compensated for by printing on a softer paper. But the usual preference is to shorten the developing time, which has a measurable affect on the higher densities in the negative. (See also Question 118) The density range in the negative can be reduced to normal in this way. Shortening the developing time, therefore, makes the slope of the characteristic curve less steep. By understanding the "brightness range" principle and the concept that black and white emulsions will record only those light values which fall roughly within a 1:64 ratio (given standard development), the photographer will be able to recognize and master most situations involving difficult exposures.

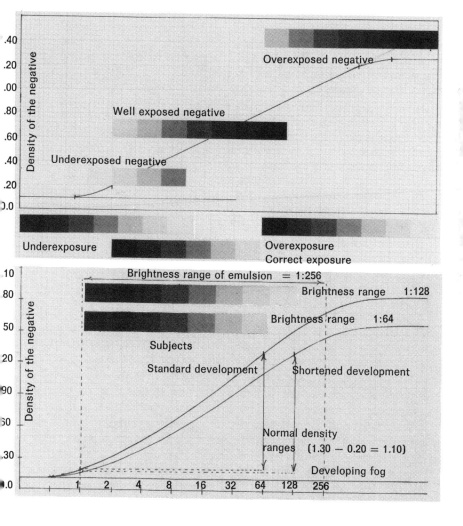

116

What is the best way to establish the brightness range of a subject?

The light meter can be of help here. Too often there is a tendency to restrict its use to the measurement of a simple aperture/shutter speed setting. One forgets that the meter can also be used to **analyze** the subject in terms of its brightness range. Naturally only a **reflected-light** exposure meter can be used in this way. Most meter scales are calibrated in arbitrary units running from 1 to 22. Each division represents a doubling of the registered light value as you move up the scale, just like the aperture system (f/22, f/16, f/11 f/8, etc.). A few precautions are called for. Most non-built-in meters have a reading angle of about 30 degrees. If the reading surface is small, the meter has to be held about 6 inches away from the subject; you must be careful not to let your hand, or the meter, throw a shadow on the surface being photographed.

By watching the meter needle you can analyze and compare diffrerent values in the scene. If there is a 1 division difference, there is twice as much reflected light; 2 divisions, 4 times the reflected light, and so forth. It is most important to measure the brightness range of the subject. To do so, point the meter at a central part of the scene which is the lightest, most directly lit (a white shirt, for example). Then measure another important feature that is dark and in shadow. Calculate the brightness range in the following way. Suppose that the first reading was 17 and the second 12; this gives a difference of 5 (equivalent to 5 stops). Applying what we learned earlier, raise 2 to the power of 5 to get 32, which is the brightness range in question.

12 13 14 15 16 17 = 1:32
  x2 x2 x2 x2 x2

In this hypothetical example, the subject's brightness range, 1:32, falls within that of the emulsion. Therefore, all the values concerned will be correctly recorded. The correct exposure will be the one indicated opposite 14 on the scale (with black and white you expose for the shadows).

The following table gives brightness ranges for a number of common situations:

Subject	Brightness range
— Panoramic landscape with haze (no foreground)	1:4
— Panoramic landscape with haze (with foreground)	1:16
— Sunny landscape (no foreground)	1:32
— Sunny street scene (with darker buildings)	1:150
— Interior (fluorescent lighting) with a window looking out on a sunny exterior	1:2000
— Same interior, with no window in view	1:64
— Sunlit face (light hair)	1:16
— Sunlit face (dark hair)	1:32

117 What is a "zone system"?

As the photographer prepares to shoot a certain scene, he must **visualize** the finished photo in his mind's eye. In particular, he must consider how he will render the light and colour values of the scene into grey tones. Will he reproduce these values naturalistically, or will he modify them and give them a subjective interpretation?

The spirit behind this creative approach to photography is often associated with the work of the celebrated photographer Ansel Adams. Certain technical controls can be put at the service of this subjective approach, namely, the aperture/shutter speed combination and the developing time. A number of tests have to be run before the "zone system" can be implemented. There is one restriction of this system: it is really meant for large format work in which each negative is treated separately. Application to a complete roll of film requires some adjustments. Nevertheless, even with such modification, it is a valuable aid when dealing with exposure problems.

From the entire range of black and white densities found on photographic paper, 9 values or zones[1] have been selected and catagorized. Each one represents a natural tone rendered into a grey value: thus, a sunlit face corresponds photographically to zone VI, foliage to zone IV, etc. Moreover, each zone as measured on a light meter represents twice the illumination of the former; the face of zone VI reflects 4 times as much light as the foliage of zone IV. There is, however, little more than a ½ stop difference between zones VII and VIII. Zone IX cannot usually be measured. Any specular reflection on glass, water or metal normally falls into this zone and has the same value as pure white paper.

Zone I: Deepest black.

Zone II: The darkest part of the image in which one can still detect texture.

Zone III: Dark surfaces with full texture.

Zone IV: Dark foliage. Portion of the face in shadow in a sunlit portrait.

Zone V: Clear northern sky — tanned skin — neutral grey card (18% reflection).

Zone VI: Average skin (Caucasian).

Zone VII: Very light skin. Pale grey objects. Snow in oblique light. Whites with delicate texture and modulations.

Zone VIII: Whites without texture — snow in direct light.

Zone IX: Pure white — specular reflections.

In the next question we will look at how the system works in practice.

---

[1] There are differences in the zone values found in Ansel Adam's version of the system, as opposed to that of Minor White. I think the latter's conform more closely to actuallity.

118 How is a light meter used in connection with the zone system?

There is a close relationship between the subject's brightness range, the brightness range of the emulsion and the zone system.

Main features of the zone system[1] fall basically under two headings:

a) The exposure (aperture/shutter speed combination). The exposure determines the **general density** of the negative and in particular assures the recording of detail in shadows or darker areas (zones II or III). "Expose for the shadows..." is the golden rule for the photographer working in black and white.

b) The developing time. A developed negative has certain minimum and maximum densities. The difference between these two values, called the **density range,** determines the degree of contrast in the negative and the grade of paper which must be used for printing. Varying the developing time has a strong effect on the higher densities, but has little effect on the lower densities. This then provides an effective means for controlling the contrast of the negative. What is its usefulness? When you photograph a scene with a very wide light range (1:28 or more), you usually get a negative that is too contrasty. But you get a more "normal" negative by proportional reduction of the developing time. The golden rule mentioned above finishes by saying "... and develop for the highlights" (that is, for the density range).

The reader may still be confused, even after consulting the suggested reference books. According to the zone system, a face in shadow falls into zone IV, while that part of the face which is in the light is assigned a zone VI value. The value of the shadow is completely variable and dependent on the nature of the lighting. With very diffuse lighting, which is entirely reflected, there will be no shadows at all, while with strong directional lighting and without fill light, the value of the skin shadow may dip to zone III or even II.

There is, therefore, a possibility of error if you base your exposure on these values. The best way to proceed is in the following two stages:

[1] For a complete description of the zone system, see white, M., **Zone System Manual,** Morgon & Morgan, or Adams, A., **The Negative,** Morgan & Morgan.

a) First establish the exposure on the basis of the **large shadows**. These should be placed in either zone II or zone III, depending on whether you want just a trace of detail (zone II) or fairly good texture (zone III). To do so, **expose for zone V.** For example: the light meter indicates a value of 12 for an article of dark clothing, which means f/5.6 at 1/30 sec. If you place this value in zone II, then the real exposure, for zone V, will be f/16 at 1/30 sec., that is, 3 stops less. If you want to capture still more texture, place it in zone III and, exposing again for zone V, we get f/11 at 1/30 sec. (2 stops less).

It may seem surprising and inconsistent at first glance to say that you should expose for the shadows and then, after measuring the luminosity of these shadows which fall into zones II or III, expose for zone V, whose value is less than the reading taken directly from these shadows. This happens because light meters are **calibrated** in relation to a grey of 18% reflectance, which represents the **average value** of the majority of scenes photographed. By exposing for zone V, therefore, you are assuring that the darker values corresponding to zones IV, III and II will be properly recorded on the negative, as will the lighter values corresponding to zones VI, VII and VIII.

b) Next, you must determine the optimum developing time by measuring the brightness range of the subject with a light meter. Take a reading of the main bright values. The difference between that reading and the one made for the shadows must not exceed a **maximum** of 6 stops (brilliancy range 1:64) for placement in zone II and 5 stops (1:32) for placement in zone III[2]. For example: the meter reads 18 (f/16, 1/250) on a white shirt, and 12 for the shadows (using zone II). There is a 6-stop difference, so developing will be standard.

---

[2] These values are only approximate, because they are based on a number of personnal parameters. Each individual will have to make his own modifications to suit his particular way of working.

119 What can be done if the brightness range of the subject is too little or too great?

■ ■

In the vocabulary of the zone system, the problem can be phrased this way: after placing the large shadows in zone III (which corresponds to the lower end of the rectilinear part of the characteristic curve), the light meter tells us that the highlights either exceed, or fall short of, zone VIII. This is what to do in each case:

The highlights exceed zone VIII: If you develop the negative normally, it will be too contrasty and have too wide a density range to be printed on No. 2 paper. First solution: use a softer paper like a No. 1 or No. 0, depending on the degree of contrast. Second solution: using the zone system, reduce developing time to tone down the contrast of the negative and bring the highlights within zone VIII, then print on No. 2 paper. This is where tests are needed to determine how a reduction in development time will achieve the desired result.

The highlights fall short of zone VIII: After placing the shadows in zone III and exposing for zone V, you can:

a) Develop normally and print on No. 2 paper if you do not want whites corresponding to zones VIII and IX.

b) Develop normally and print on No. 3 or 4 paper if you want to recover the whole 9-zone range. It may not be possible to do so if the subject's brightness range is very narrow, as is the case with a landscape during a snowstorm, for example.

c) Increase the developing time (up to 100%) and print on No. 2 or No. 3 paper, depending on the contrast desired. This is the zone system solution.

Although you always expose for the shadows in black and white photographs, the preceding shows that **developing is based on the highlights,** and that the idea is to produce negatives in which the density range (contrast) allows enlarging on No. 2 paper.

You may protest, quite rightly too, that most light meters are not constructed for detailed analysis of a scene. How do you get a reading for a distant landscape enshrouded in haze? In this case only an over-all reading is possible. But it is easy to understand that such a scene has a very narrow brightness range; it includes as little as 1:4, or scarcely 3 zones. You will therefore not go wrong if you **reduce** the exposure by a value of 1 or 2 stops over the actual reading of the light meter and increase the developing time by 50 to 100% (these values are only approximate because they depend on many different parameters).

On the left, an exposure from average reading of reflected light and standard development. On the right, the exposure is reduced by 2 stops and developing time is doubled. Both photos were printed on the same grade of paper. There is an appreciable increase in the contrast.

120 Are there any additional guidelines which can be drawn from the zone system?

Yes, but only if you understand the process of **placing** the exposure, and the role of developing in the **expansion** or **contraction** of the values of the subject through the negative's density range.

If you find yourself with a roll of film which contains scenes with differing brightness ranges (zone numbers), you will have to develop for the majority of exposures with the same value. These can be printed on No. 2 paper. The others can be adjusted by using a softer or harder paper. As you shoot, make a note on each roll about developing requirements (standard, shorter or longer).

With diffuse lighting (sun obscured, cloudy weather, reflected light, ceiling with fluorescent bulbs), the brightness range of the subject usually permits standard development. Placement of the shadows in zone III (or II) will automatically be taken care of if you use one of the following methods:

a) Incident-light exposure meter: Point the meter towards the camera and use the exposure indicated. The reading is automatically made for zone V (18% grey).

b) Reflected-light exposure meter: There are three possibilities. 1) Take an overall reading if the subject displays values running from white to black. 2) Take a reading on a neutral density card. 3) Take a reading on the palm of the hand: it has a reflectance of about 35%, or twice that of the neutral density card. It therefore falls into zone VI. To get the correct exposure (zone V), you must double the exposure time, that is **open up** one stop.

Although this zone-V exposure method for use with the two types of meter will often give acceptable results, neither method of reading gives us any information on the brightness range of the subject (the number of zones). If it exceeds 1:128, the methods discussed above may lead to an underexposure.

Therefore, whenever the lighting is directional or contrasty, or the photographer does not have time to analyze the subject with his light meter, or cannot get near it, the following procedure should give good general results:

a) To calculate the exposure: Take a reading on the palm of the hand, making sure that it is not lit directly. **Double** the exposure indicated by the meter.

b) To calculate the length of developing: take a reading off the palm of the hand while it is lit directly. If the difference between the two readings is in the order of one or two stops, you can develop normally. If there is a difference of three or four stops, the developing time should be reduced by 15% to 30%.

Once again, many factors play a part in this complex process.

One example, which unfortunately is all too common: a lens covered with dust and fingerprints reduces the contrast of the negative considerably. Distance of the subject from the camera has the same effect because of the phenomenon of aerial perspective. This is why shots taken with a telephoto often lack contrast.

Consequently, you must take a critical look at your negative and, working from the golden rule mentioned earlier, discover for yourself what modifications you should make.

121 Could you review the key points from the articles dealing with the problem of exposure?

The density of the negative results from blackening which is triggered by light and completed by the developer.

The density range of the negative generally indicates its contrast.

A **normal** negative has a density range of about 1:10 and can be printed on No. 2 paper.

One negative can have different density margins depending on whether a condenser-type enlarger is used.

Every scene contains a variable number of light regions.

The ratio of the minimum and maximum light values is called the brightness range.

The greater the brightness range of the subject, the more precise the exposure estimate must be.

Photography is a record of corresponding light densities provided by a scene.

Every emulsion is limited in the number of different light values it can record by some maximum density.

The brightness range of an emulsion and the corresponding variations in density are represented graphically by the characteristic curve.

The brightness range of an emulsion can reach 1:250.

Shooting two subjects with different brightness ranges and then developing them the same way will produce negatives with different density ranges; the wider density range will go with the scene that has the greater brightness range.

Whenever a subject has a brightness range of about 1:64 (a difference of six stops between the most extreme values), developing will usually be standard. Whenever this range exceeds 1:128, the developing time must be shortened. It is usually increased when the range is below 1:64.

A reflected-light exposure meter can be used to analyze a subject. Each 1-division reading increase indicates a doubling of the reflected light.

The zone system is, in its inventor's own terms, a technical tool for pre-visualizing the finished photographic product.

The reflected-light exposure meter is the basic working instrument of the system.

Meters are calibrated on the basis of the 18% neutral gray

factor (zone V).

The photographer must undertake many exposure, developing and printing tests before he will have a thorough knowledge and control of his material.

The range of values of photographic paper is divided into 9 different zones which extend from pure white to pure black.

These zones correspond to the range of different densities situated on the rectilinear part of the characteristic curve.

The rule "expose for the shadows" also applies to the zone system.

The term "placing" a particular subject in a given zone means that you intend to render the part in question by the grey value attributed to this zone.

Zone III represents the grey value that a well-detailed shadow should have.

Zone VII represents the grey value that a delicately textured bright part should have.

You **place** strong shadows in zone III and **expose** for zone V.

Under these conditions, if the light meter indicates that the highlights fall into zone VIII, developing will be normal. It will be shorter if they exceed it and longer if they fall short: develop for the highlights.

Use of different grades of paper is compatible with the zone system and allows for more nuances.

122 Why did a black and white emulsion that I exposed for five seconds, as the meter indicated, still give an underexposed negative?

When you take a reading with a light meter, you get a whole series of possible aperture/shutter speed combinations. For example, in sunny weather a Plus-X, 125 ASA film will give the following combinations:

f/22 f/16 f/11 f/8 f/5.6
1/60 1/125 1/250 1/500 1/1000

We know that any of these combinations will produce a normal negative. Without being aware of it, we have just applied a principle known to photographers as the law of reciprocity.

When the light level is low, we might get the following series of readings from the meter:

f/8   f/5.6   f/4
8 sec. 4 sec.   ¼ sec.
    f/2.8   f/2   f/1.4
    1 sec. ½ sec.   ¼ sec.

You would tend to think that an exposure of four seconds at f/5.6 would produce the same negative as an exposure of ¼ sec. at f/1.4. In fact it does not: the negative shot at ¼ sec., f/1.4 will be well exposed, while at four seconds, f/5.6 it will be considerably underexposed. This involves an **exception to the law of reciprocity.** Whenever the exposure exceeds one second,

there is an effective lowering in the sensitivity or ASA of the emulsion. The exposure must therefore be longer than that indicated on the light meter.

This phenomenon applies in general to black and white emulsions which are exposed for longer than one second.

The table below provides some **average** corrections:

Exposure according to meter	Exposure needed
1 sec. 2 sec.	1 sec. 3 sec.
4 sec.	6½ sec.
8 sec. 15 sec.	16 sec. 35 sec.
30 sec. 1 min.	75 sec. 3 min.

To be certain, triple up your exposure; that is, take one exposure at the corrected shutter speed as recommended, another at half this speed and a third at twice the speed.

The same thing happens with colour emulsions. The manufacturers provide correction tables to which you should refer. With colour, the loss of sensitivity at low light levels will be aggravated by an imbalance in the three colour layers; this leads to the appearance of a false colour cast. For this reason, you must not only alter the exposure time but also use a compensating filter as indicated by the manufacturer.

(Photo by R.W.)

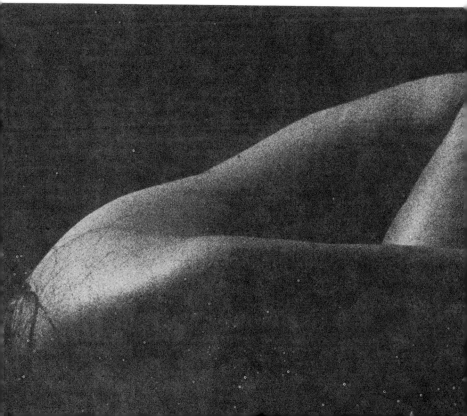

123 What are the advantages and disadvantages of the different systems used for macrophotography?

Macrophotography involves shooting small objects or parts of objects in such a way that the image size on film may vary anywhere between 1/10 and 10 times the real size.

There are four different system in use: close-up lens, extension tube, bellows and "special" lens. The close-up lens is simply attached to the front of the camera lens like a filter. It is classified by its power in dioptres, which in turn is related to the focal length.

1 dioptre = 1000mm focal length
2 dioptres = 500mm focal length
3 dioptres = 333mm focal length, etc.

A 3-dioptre lens magnifies 3 times more than a 1-dioptre lens. It allows you to get **much closer** to the subject than with a regular lens. The greater the dioptric power, the closer the camera can be moved to a subject (with 3 dioptres, and the lens focussed at 2 ft., the real distance from the object to the lens is 8¼ inches). But the scale of magnification will scarcely exceed 35% with a 5-dioptre lens; beyond this limit there is a noticable degradation of the image.

Advantages: Minimal cost (a few dollars), easy to handle, no need to change the exposure. **Disadvantages:** Fairly sharp image when the aperture is small, but degradation of the image increases with the power of the lens.

Extension tubes and bellows have a number of points in common: they are both mounted between the lens and the camera body. They increase the film-lens distance and thus permit closer shooting and a larger image. Lenses of different focal lengths may be used with both systems. For a given lens-film distance, the shortest focal length will give the greatest magnification. On the other hand, this lens will also be much closer to the object; this may be inconvenient, particularly if you have to worry about lighting. As a result, the preference is usually for lenses of 105 or 135mm (with the 24 x 36 format camera).

The basic difference between the two systems lies in the fact that the bellows allows smooth and **continuous** increase in the magnification, while the tubes are limited to fixed and discontinuous changes (there are usuallly 3 to 5 tubes).

Advantages: Because there is no optical intermediary involved, the specifications of the original lens remain unchanged. Images are larger than life and of high quality.

Disadvantages: Bellows and tubes can only be used with SLR cameras. They permit some light loss which must be made up in the exposure. They are awkward to handle and are relatively expensive: $25 for a set of tubes; $40 to $125 for bellows.

The "special" lens allows continuous focussing from infinity to a few inches. The Micro Nikkor lens has a 55mm focal length, its closest focussing is from infinity to a few inches, and its maximum magnification is 50%, with tube — 100%.

Advantages: Designed for close-ups, excellent optical quality. Auto-correcting for light loss.

Disadvantages: Limited maximum aperture (f/3.5). Cannot therefore replace the standard lens, which is usually much faster. Cannot exceed magnification of 1.0.

A Hasselblad with an 80 mm lens and bellows sunshade is very good for eliminating stray light.

124 What are the shooting peculiarities of macro-photography?

Depth of field. When you are working very close to the subject, the depth of field is considerably reduced. For example: with a 5-dioptre lens, focussing at 2 ft, the real distance of the subject is 6½ in., and the depth of field at f/8 is only ¼ in. Consequently, you normally work with a small aperture, increase the shutter speed and use a tripod.

Scale of magnification (M). With the camera in position and focussed, place a ruler (preferably metric) in front of the object. Look through the viewfinder, and line up the zero end of the ruler with the left-hand edge of the frame. Note the distance measured to the right-hand edge. This represents the width of the image (say 51mm). Knowing that the negative measures 36mm in width, you divide 36 by 51 to get 0.7, which is the magnification desired.

Again, with the camera set up and focussed, you can measure the distance "V" (the film-lens or "image" distance) and apply the formula

$$M = \frac{V}{F} - 1, \text{ where "F"}$$

is the focal length of the lens. To find the extension of bellows or tubes necessary for taking in a pre-determined space, measure the space that you want included on the negative. Then divide 36mm (the width of the negative) by the width of the space in question (also in mm). This gives us the magnification M. Then simply apply a formula related to the one mentioned above: $V = F(M+1) - F$. The rsult represents the **extra** extension required. Once the bellows (or tubes) have been' set up and adjusted to this length, you no longer touch the focussing ring but rather move **the whole unit** back and forth until the image is sharp.

To find the exposure coefficient to compensate for the light loss caused by an increase in the film-lens (image) distance, open the diaphragm, increase the length of the exposure or bring the light source closer (flash, for example). It is generally preferable to work with a small aperture in order to preserve the depth of field. Always begin with a **normal** aperture/shutter speed combination from the light meter, then correct according to the following table:

Multiply the distance of the flash (or aperture stop) by:	.8	.65	.5	.4	.3	.25	.2	.17	.14
For magnification of: ·	.2	.5	1.0	1.5	2.0	3.0	4.0	5.0	6.0
Or multiply the exposure time by:	1.5	2.25	4	6	9	16	25	35	50

Remember, if the corrected exposure time exceeds 1 sec., you must make a further correction because of the reciprocity problem (see correction table, Question 122).

Note: built-in light meters may not be precise enough for macrophotography, so it is best to check yours with a few tests.

(Photo by R.W.)

125 What is the distinction among the terms "close up", "macrophotography" and "microphotography"?

If the ratio of reproduction between a subject and an image is approximately 10 to 1, you have produced a conventional "close up" photo. A normal lens at a distance of about three feet usually produces an image which is 1/10 the size of the subject.

If the ratio of reproduction between a subject and an image is **less** than 10 to 1, you have entered the world of "macrophotography". Moreover, when the ratio is 1 to 1, the subject size is equal to the image. For example, if an eye measuring one inch is photographed to produce an image measuring exactly one inch, the result is a "life size" representation.

Below the subject-image ratio of 1 to 1, macrophotography with all of its gadgets permits magnification in the order of 20 to 25 times the subject's size.

If the photo image is 25 to 100,000 times the size of the subject, you are working with microscopes to produce "microphotography".

To do macrophotography you require a close-up lens, extension tubes or, better still, bellows, along with (budget permitting) a circular flash.

For a while the beginner will be content with a close-up lens. This will allow him to shoot at distances from three feet to five inches. Later he may be attracted to extension tubes, which give only fixed magnification. Bellows, however, allow variable magnification and, like extension tubes, may be used with different lenses.

This kind of work cannot, of course, be done hand-held. Given that the depth of field is practically non-existent (around 1/100 in.), the diaphragm should always be set at f/22 or f/32. This means slow shutter speeds and therefore the use of a tripod.

The magnification ratios and corresponding corrections are clearly indicated on the bellows focussing rack. The need to stop down means fairly strong lighting. The two best sources of light are the sun and flash since their colour temperature is always stable. In the sun you will need a reflector for fill light, made of white cardboard or aluminum foil.

Through-the-lens metering is a distinct advantage in macrophotography.

While most enthusiasts of macrophotography use a normal lens, there is a growing demand for the "macro" lens, which is designed especially for macrophotography. These lenses offer a magnification ratio from 1.1 to infinity, and they carry their own extension tubes.

Bellows for the Zenit-E.

Extension tube.

126 I have always dreamed of getting a "press card". Where and how can I get one?

I have a feeling that this page is going to disappoint some of you. Every beginner (including me) has dreamed of getting hold of one of these cards, this "badge" which supposedly opens all doors. Well, prepare yourself for a shock. This "golden key" does not exist.

The press card issued by a newspaper is nothing more than an **identity card.** In fact, most photographers must show their card even when they enter the premises of their own newspaper. This card, with its photograph, is no more special than the ID cards given to the employees of any factory.

In the case of some special event, such as the arrival of a dignitary at the airport, the opening of a session of parliament, a hockey game, an MP's speaking tour, etc., the officials involved issue a series of passes for the press people who will be covering the event. The passes are valid only for the duration of the specified events and must be destroyed afterwards. In the case of professional sports, however, a card is issued for the entire season, whether this involves hockey, baseball or any other major league activity. It is made out in the name of the newspaper, not in the name of the individual concerned.

There is a press card issued by the police to photographers and journalists. This gives them access to the courts and city hall, but nowhere else.

No, that miraculous all-purpose card is only a figment of people's imagination. The only way to get to the action is to be bold and determined. Push, push . . . and ask questions **later.**

The golden key. . .?

127 Is there a simple way to distort an image when you shoot, other than the trick of turning up a corner of the printing paper as you enlarge?

■ ■

An important photographer by the name of Weegee kept a whole generation of photographers breathless with his amazing distorted images. Although unwilling, he finally divulged his secret. The trick amounted to nothing more than placing a sheet of plastic (about 4 in. wide and 1/8 in. thick), which had been softened over a hot burner, in front of the lens. The deformed plastic contorts the image into weird and unusual shapes. For example, it will stretch the body of a horse by three or four feet, or give a menacing look to the Mona Lisa, and so on.

This technique is used in the cinema as well as in still photography.

Armed with his secret, Weegee (a press photographer) jokingly pretended to be "5000 years ahead of his time", but pulled off some really exceptional examples of photographic "magic".

There are many techniques for distorting an image. For example, bend a ferrotype plate in different ways and photograph people on it. You might also shoot through rippled glass.

The plastic softens up quickly over an element.

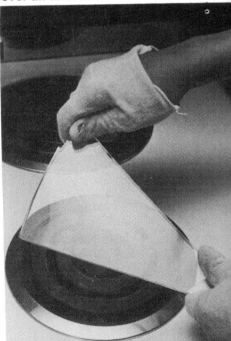

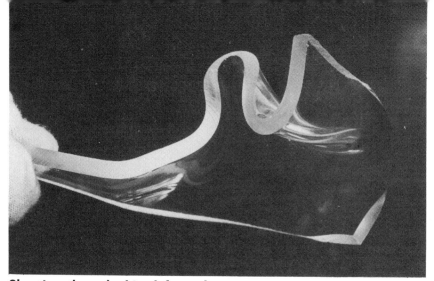

Shooting through this deformed plastic will produce some very strange images.

As good as gold one minute... ...a little monkey the next.

128 What are the basic rules for putting together a photographic report? Is telling a story on film more appropriate to the cinema?

Whether it is cinematic or not, the story you want to tell must have a **beginning, a middle and an end.**

You will probably be working with people. Your photos will have to give a maximum amount of information about what these people are like: their habits, ways of dressing, how they fit into their own environment. Posed photos are inadvisable for a report such as this. If, however, you happen to witness an unusual scene, but are not ready to shoot it, try to recreate it and make the situation look as "normal" as possible.

We photographers sometimes forget that our work is **visual** and depends not on words or drawings but on photographic images. We are story-tellers in images.

Composition plays an important role in these images. Framing, the centre of interest, the rhythm, the right balance of shapes and masses, be they symmetrical or asymmetrical (preferably the latter), balance, harmony, unity, the perspective, etc., not to mention the rule of thirds, are among the elements which must be considered if the photo is to be pleasing to the eye. The interested reader should consult my book **Techniques in Photography** which treats this matter in some depth.

We live in a cinematic world where everything is in constant motion. The photographer's role, which is sometimes rather frustrating since he is not a film-maker, is to capture images "on the move" and reproduce them in a static state. If the photographer manages to give an impression of "movement", he has achieved a dimension which gives life to his artistic message.

Before setting to work, the photographer must research his subject thoroughly and obtain all the pertinent information he can on the people involved, the place and so forth. He might examine post cards or travel posters of the place in question, or read about the lifestyle of the people.

It is a good idea to take a few long shots first, then some medium shots and finally some close-ups. This goes for both landscapes and people. Use of the telephoto will prove indispensable.

I have already emphasized the importance of varying the shooting angle. Try shooting from floor level or from up high. Pay no attention to those who say this is not the way people "normally" look at things . . . that no one gets down on all fours to look (except maybe burglars). But if it will give you dynamic pictures, why not?

One important quality that every press or reporter-photographer must have is the ability to anticipate the unexpected. As a situation unfolds, you should be able to judge which direction it is apt to go next. Always be prepared. Aperture, shutter speed preset to suit the lighting conditions, focus on the hyperfocal, except of course for telephotos, and never, never be stingy with the film. If you are at the 27th or 28th frame and you have a feeling that something is about to happen, change the film right away, fast.

If you're working in colour and your slides are going to be used for 4-colour reproduction, you must make sure to get the correct exposure. Wherever possible, therefore, triple up your shots: one according to the meter, one a stop over and another a stop under. The ideal thing is to shoot with a negative colour film, **overexpose** 1 stop and, if necessary, have slides or black & white prints run off afterwards.

At this stage, the photographer who is even slightly serious about his work will put aside the rules (you know, shoot only between 10 a.m. and 3 p.m.), and throw himself into shooting early in the morning and late in the afternoon, and by so doing is likely to get much more sophisticated results.

If the situation requires flash, do not hesitate but try to use it indirectly by bouncing it off ceilings, walls and other reflective surfaces.

Continued overleaf

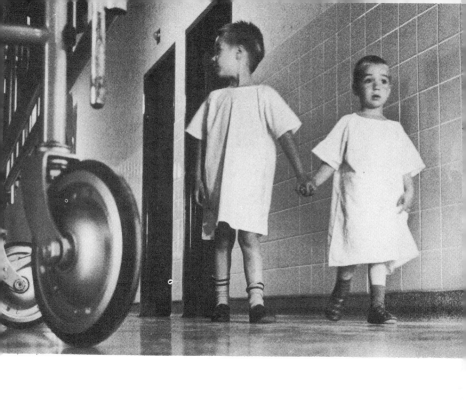

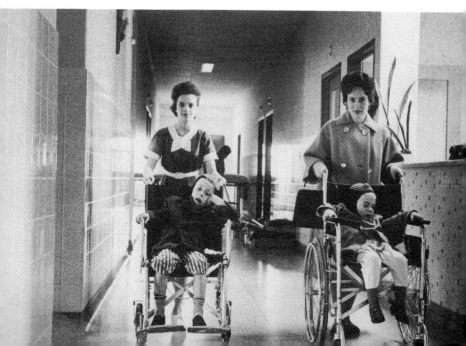

129 Why did you not provide technical data on the photos you published in your first book, as they do in the specialized magazines?

I am always dubious about giving this kind of information to the reader, because I consider it a waste of time and, in some respects, even misleading.

You will appreciate why after the following explanation: if I tell you that a photo was shot at 1/125 sec. and f/8, with Panatomic X film, I am not telling you the whole truth. The magazines rarely give you any more information than that.

I ought to add the time of day at which the photo was shot, the type of sky or the nature of the lighting, the focal length of the lens used, the make of camera, the type of filter used, the developer, and a note about whether or not the photo was deliberately under-or overexposed. You can see that the information is far from complete. And by omitting all these details, I stand a good chance of leading you astray.

The only time the inclusion of technical data can be justified is perhaps when the photographer uses a piece of special equipment, like a fish-eye lens, or resorts to some special technique.

It would be naive for another photographer to try to recreate a picture by following the technical data provided at the bottom of a published photo. Moreover, many photographers forget exactly what their exposure was and give only approximate information. In other words, do not trust this technical information!

Technical data for this photo: Nikon camera — 105 mm lens — Tri-X film — 800 ASA — Honeywell electronic flash — guide number 160 — flash at 4 ft bounced off white ceiling — the old lady's hands 6 ft from the ceiling — 1/60 sec. at f/16 — deliberately underexposed — D-76 developer, 8 min. at 70 °F (21 °C) — deliberately overdeveloped to bring up the contrast in the hands and reduce detail in the dress — printed on Brovira No. 4, burning-in on the dress to accentuate the hands.

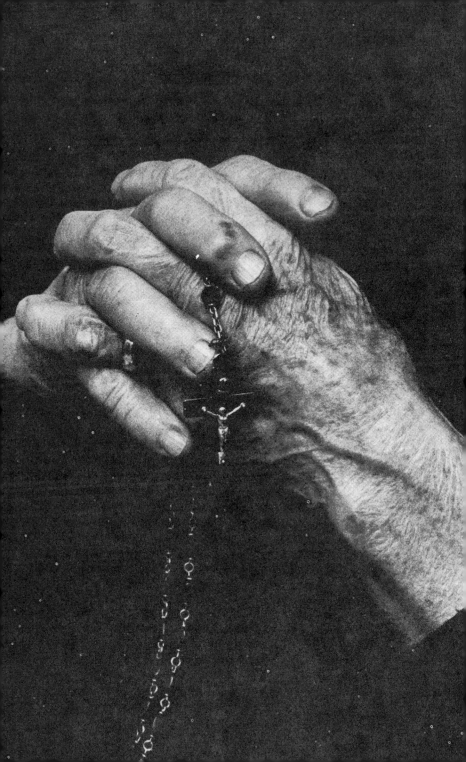

130 What is meant by "hyperfocal"? Do 35mm reflex cameras have this quality?

Box cameras, Instamatics and other cameras costing less than $50 are made in such a way that the focussing of their lens is fixed on the hyperfocal distance. The hyperfocal distance is the shortest distance which allows a clear sharp image when the lens is focussed on infinity. In other words, the hyperfocal distance is that which gives the greatest depth of field, starting at infinity.

Here we are talking, of course, about a **fixed diaphragm,** as found on the cameras mentioned above (about f/11).

For cameras with an adjustable diaphragm, this distance gets much closer as you stop down.

Press photographers often use the hyperfocal when a confused or rapid series of events makes focussing too difficult.

For a 28 or 35mm wide-angle camera, the hyperfocal is around 15 feet at f/11 or f/8. This means that from 10 feet to infinity, everything is in focus.

If you have a camera whose lens is outfitted with a depth of field scale, it is easy to make use of the hyperfocal. Here is all you do. As you can see in the photos opposite, lenses have a reference mark (usually a little arrow or a black or red dot) to tell you where you are. The focussing ring is turned to the right until it reaches infinity. The aperture ring is turned to the right until it reaches the smallest aperture (f/16 or f/22). This point is called the index. On certain lenses, there is a series of little lines or aperture numbers on either side of this index. These lines or numbers serve to indicate the depth of field on the distance scale of the focussing ring. Assuming that the infinity sign is at the index and the aperture at f/16, it is simply a matter then of turning the focussing ring until the infinity sign stops at the f/16 mark **on the depth of field scale.** Then the index will no longer be opposite infinity, but rather opposite a certain number of feet, and this number is the hyperfocal. I think it will become clear when you try it out on your own equipment.

With a standard 52 mm lens, at infinity, f/16, depth of field 25 ft. to infinity.

With the infinity mark at the last line on the depth of field scale, on the left, you are "on the hyperfocal". Here it is about 23 ft.

Focussing at infinity, aperture at f/8, depth of field 10 ft to infinity.

With the infinity mark at f/8 on the depth of field scale, 10 ft becomes the hyperfocal distance.

131 I have in my possession a large number of excellent photographs. Can I sell them to an agency, and for how much?

This is a question which preoccupies many amateur photographers — and for good reason! After investing a sizeable amount of money in equipment and setting up a printing lab, nothing could be more natural than wanting to make this pastime profitable by selling a few photographs.

Speaking only for the province of Quebec, to my knowledge, there is no photo agency or decent photo-library. There is a tremendous demand for photographs, from magazines, newspapers, ad agencies, educational organizations, etc., and yet, they cannot come to any central clearing house for help. Hopefully, this situation is only temporary, and that we soon will be able to draw on the work of the many serious amateurs who have been looking for just such an outlet.

In the meantime, I would suggest that you take one or two dozen photos, 8 x 10's or, at the most, 11 x 14's to every serious magazine editor you can find. Although they will not all be in a position to buy pictures from you, it is worth taking the trouble to visit as many as you can.

When you consider all the popular and specialized magazines, the daily newspapers, the weeklies and the publications of various private and public organizations, there is a large potential market for photographs.

Naturally these potential clients will look very critically at the photos submitted to them, which means they must be of really professional quality.

As far as the price they will pay is concerned, it is very difficult to give an accurate estimate. There is no scale of fees or other index to act as a guide here. I can only give a few examples, which must not, of course, be taken as definitive. For example, most dailies pay from $5 to $8 for each black & white photo published (this, in my opinion, is too little). Maclean's pays $35 for a black and white photo. Some magazines will pay $50 for a colour photo published on the inside pages and up to $300 for a colour photo used on the cover.

A Quebec landscape.

132 I have in my possession a very special photograph. How can I have it permanently copyrighted?

The business of copyright with regard to photographs has been, and probably always will be, in a chaotic state.

If you have created a photograph worthy of being protected under copyright, then the patent office in Ottawa will give you a copyright number which is dated and accompanied by a small "c" in a circle — ©. It will cost only $3, but you must request this . . .

You may receive a good price for having it published, but the protection on it will probably only cover its initial use. Don't be surprised if, some time later, someone else tries to use it (or does use it) without your permission. There would be little point in taking the person or company concerned to court: the legal fees and time it would consume could be ruinous. The general situation in publishing, magazines and newspapers is chaotic as far as pictorial copyright is concerned. We are witness every day to the most flagrant plagiarism, with photos being stolen from under the nose of the owner. A photographer might get some satisfaction in court, but this kind of thing almost never comes to trial.

A handful of good magazines really respect photo ownership. If they use a photo of yours a second time, they are good about sending a cheque without having to be prompted. Second use normally commands about 50% of the original fee. Although virtually all periodicals give notice somewhere that their pictures and text are protected by copyright ("all rights reserved"), this means little in practice. It may scare off the "uninitiated"; but the real pirates of the trade, who know that the copyright laws have no teeth, are not prevented from shameless "borrowing".

133 What basic equipment would you recommend for shooting hockey, baseball or football games, and how would I go about selling the photographs?

First of all you must realize that all the large magazines and newspapers always assign a reporter and a photographer to cover such sporting events.

You have undoubtedly noticed these journalists and photographers sitting, by the edge of the rink or field where they are permitted to roam freely. Needless to say, they have been issued with a special permit, and no amateur, however serious, would stand a chance of getting one (see Question 126).

Sports pictures are normally done in black & white, but there is an increasing demand for colour these days.

Most photographers use a motor-driven Nikon, which allows them to photograph rapid action at the rate of 3 frames a second. If your pictures are not as spectacular as the professional ones, don't worry . . . it is probably the motor drive which makes the difference (see Question 134).

Since these photographers are working quite close to the action, they use a 35 or 52mm lens in order to cover the play effectively. They may have an 85 or 105mm lens on their second camera (they always have two), to enable them to get close-ups as well, but they rarely use any longer lenses.

The lighting at the Montreal Forum, for example, has been boosted enough to allow the CBC to televise in colour, which means that photographers can work at 1/1000 sec. at f/8 — f/5.6 **without flash** (Tri-X, 800 ASA). Anybody using flash is working in colour.

Even if you have to sit twenty rows back, you can still do all the shooting you like, although you will be better off with a 200mm lens.

If you manage to get a really **exceptional** picture a newspaper will be glad to give you a good price for it, but you will have to be quick about it. The newspapers often come out very soon after the end of a game (see Question 131).

The best approach for the amateur is to get in touch with the editor of a small suburban weekly. If you manage to convince him that you are the ideal man for the job, he might send you out to cover some of the local amateur sporting events. Show him a dozen of your best pictures. Who knows? Every photographer got his start in this modest way.

It is up to your editor to get you a pass to the restricted areas around the rink or playing field. In a few years, perhaps we will find you in the front row at the N.H.L.!

A Montreal Alouettes work-out.

134

Buying a motor for my Minolta represents a large expenditure. Would it be a good investment if I do a lot of sports photography?

■■■■■■■■■■■■■■■■■■■■■■■■■■

The first motor drives for still cameras appeared about ten years ago and they are growing more popular all the time.

Anyone who purchases such a piece of equipment is really putting himself in a privileged position. I would encourage the purchase of a motor particularly if you are specializing in sports. The manufacturers have designed these motors with action photography in mind. Handling the camera becomes a lot simpler with a motor attachment, because the motor takes over the functions of cocking the shutter and advancing the film. All that is necessary is to press down on the shutter-release, and keep pressing down. You can shoot at a rate of three or four frames a second, faster than any photographer could possibly shoot manually.

During the winter, cold weather brings the speed of a four-frames-per-second motor down to three frames. But can you imagine a motor opening and closing the shutter (not to mention raising and lowering the mirror) 180 times a minute? Needless to say, a camera has to be extremely well built to withstand such heavy use day after day. I envy the position you are in, because the Minolta motor (the SR-M I believe) is perhaps the only one which features automatic rewinding.

This can be a tremendous advantage in situations where you have no time to lose. Imagine trying to blink your eyes 250 times in less than 85 seconds. That is what your camera will do for you. It makes the line between still photography and the cinema thinner than ever . . .

As a press photographer, however, I must say that I often hesitate to use a motor drive if a shot must be taken at a very precise moment (like the arrival of race horses at the wire, or a skier hitting the finishing line at 50 or 60 feet a second). I would be worried — and it does happen often enough — that I would get two shots, one just before the moment of arrival and another just after.

A photographer who works without a motor but knows what he is doing, may have a better chance of getting the right shot than one shooting at three or four frames a second.

The motor may get a lot more shots, yet miss the split second climactic moment. Moreover, there is the danger of running out of film much more quickly since the motor really gobbles it up.

By transforming your still camera into something approaching a movie camera the motor does give you a greater versatility. As an example, if photographing a VIP who goes from his door to a waiting limousine in five seconds, without a motor, you would get no more than three shots, while with one you would get more like twenty.

A motor allows you to re-focus while shooting people who are moving towards you. This is especially valuable when doing portraits of children who change position and expression three times a second!

There are several different kinds of motor attachments. Practice with the camera empty at first, since the motor eats up a roll of 36 in 12 seconds. If the moment you are waiting for doesn't happen until the 13th second you will be out of luck! First, get used to working in bursts of three or four frames. You will be amazed at how much sharper your pictures are, simply because you do not have to keep working the shutter-release and thereby risk jiggling the camera.

Things really get interesting when you use the motor drive with a telephoto lens and radio-operated remote control.

One, two, three. Time elapsed — 1 second.

135 I am a taxi driver and I see a lot of automobile accidents. How do I sell photos of these accidents to a newspaper?

From time to time the name of an unknown photographer appears under an important first-page picture in the daily newspaper. This is not surprising since photography is becoming more and more a part of our daily lives. There is hardly a major event which occurs without the presence of an amateur photographer, ready to take pictures. Images of death, as they happen, are becoming as common place in our newspapers as on television. You have only to recall the assassinations of the two Kennedys, which were recorded on the spot by amateur photographers and filmmakers. A taxi driver, or anyone else who drives the streets of a big city all day, stands an excellent chance of getting exclusive pictures before the police and press people arrive.

Here are some relevant suggestions.

• Have the phone number of the city desk at three or four big newspapers close at hand.

• As soon as you have your shot, phone the newspaper which you think might be most interested.

• Explain the facts and emphasize that you have an exclusive. Identify yourself and give all the details of the accident — where it took place, the vehicles involved, injuries or fatalities. The person you talk to will have a lot of questions and you should be well prepared with your answers.

• Sometimes they will ask you to bring in the film directly or they will send out their own photographer to get it. (In either case, it is unlikely you will have time to develop it yourself.)

• Tell the photographer what ASA you shot at (he will need to tell the lab technician).

• Try whenever possible to work with Tri-X at 400 or 800 ASA.

• If you have to see the editor, you should be able to provide a list of names of those involved. Remember, a newspaper's job is to describe a situation in full — where, when, what, who, why and how.

• Always leave your name and telephone number in case they require additional details.

Remember that a picture should speak for itself. Try to make your picture explain as much as possible by including, for example, street signs or landmarks which will identify the location.

The best lesson in what makes an acceptable newspaper photograph comes from simply reading newspapers; note what kinds of pictures get published and what is said about them in the captions.

Shooting photos for newspapers in colour is a waste of time and money. Newspapers still do not have the budget to publish news photos in colour.

Speed and discriminating judgment are essential in this kind of work. Remember — old news is no news.

Taxi drivers see many accidents in the course of their work.

Here is a photo that was sold by a taxi driver to a Montreal newspaper.

136

I am always amazed at the extraordinary colour photographs which appear regularly in National Geographic Magazine. Is it a closely guarded secret how they get these results?

■■■■■■■■■■■■■■■■■■■■■■■■■■■

Rest assured that this photographic elite has no secret formula, but only an extremely refined expertise in their field. They work with the same technical resources as other photographers, but they have perfected their handling of these resources. There are perhaps one hundred photographers in the U.S. who work under the same roof at the National Geographic Society. About 30 of them are full time and the rest are part-time.

For the amateur who wants to expand his horizons, there is nothing better than to read this magazine regularly. The National Geographic produces pictures which push photographic technique to the limit. They are the result of inspired creative work. The amateur may be surprised to learn that all of it is usually shot on 35mm.

You will have noticed that the magazine does not publish anything in black and white. Each issue contains about 150 photographs, many of which are absolutely unique.

The quality is consistently high because this organization maintains the most rigorous technical and professional standards. Each photographer is given two or three foreign assignments a year (see Question 128), which may take him to the four corners of the world for over half the year. The rest of his time he spends at headquarters in Washington, D.C., working on local assignments.

In the course of these excursions the photographer will often be accompanied by approximately 1500 pounds of baggage and equipment.

National Geographic photographers are given the equipment of their choice, but the majority use Leicas, Nikkormats and Nikons, usually about five cameras each. They have at their disposal the whole range of lenses from 20 to 500mm, as well as fish-eyes and 1000mm's. They also carry three or four different kinds of electronic flash of various strengths. The whole group uses about 20,000 to 25,000 rolls of 36-frame colour film every year. Bruce Dale, my source of information at the N.G.S., admits that his favourite is Kodachrome II, and his opinion seems to be shared by the majority of his colleagues. He also likes Ektachrome and High Speed Ektachrome (daylight and type B). He adds that the N.G.S. has a collection of about 5,000,000 slides ...

The changeover from large format to 35mm took place between the years 1935 and 1945.

Bruce Dale explains that their work has to be organized to a degree which might at first seem excessive, but is in fact necessary if they are to keep track of all the complex information concerning the identification of rolls of film, the time of day the shot was taken, the place, the names of people involved, etc. All these details must be reported to Washington at the end of each working day. The photographers must stay in close contact with the editors in case more information or pictures are needed.

Let me just add in closing — and this will come as no surprise to many of you — that a mere 1% of all the photographs taken actually appear in the pages of National Geographic Magazine.

137 Can a serious young photographer who wants a career as a photo-journalist hope to become a staff member with a large metropolitan newspaper?

I do not know how many times this question has been asked of me in the last five years. The most amazing thing is that none of the young people to whom I have given the advice that I am about to repeat ever seems to have followed it. This has led me to the conclusion, perhaps a little hastily, that our youth have lost that essential prerequisite to success — perseverance.

Note first of all that a big newspaper normally does not hire experienced photographers, but prefers to train them itself. In the past ten years, our paper (*La Presse* in Montreal) has only hired four photographers (including me) and all three of the others were trained in this way.

My first word of advice would be to discourage you from filling in a job application. They are a waste of time. The young man of 18, 19 or 20 should appear for work at the paper as a messenger. If he is not hired immediately, it should not take too long; it is not a well-paid job and the turnover is rather high. Once he is hired, the young hopeful can expect to work in this job for at least a year or a year-and-a-half. If he is hardworking and ambitious, he will eventually be moved to the position of **clerk** for about a year or so. The secret is that, during this two year period, he should be pursuing his interest in photography, either covering weddings or doing various kinds of commercial work in his spare time. He should show these results to the newspaper editors whom he will know quite well by then. Sooner or later he will get posted to the dispatch room. There, for the first time, he will experience all the activities having to do with press photography. He will, for example, "receive" photos from the press agencies on the wire-photo machine, which will be a profitable experience for him. The next stage will be to get a job as a darkroom technician. Taking photographs is then just a step away.

All in all, the young messenger boy may — if the experience of the last three photographers at our newspaper is anything to go by — become a photographer in less than three years.

But, as I mentioned above, only a few potential photographers have told me that they are prepared to wait four years! It's difficult to believe . . .

Working as a photo-journalist requires a very special kind of training. The would-be photographer must be aggressive and have the ability to react quickly in a difficult situation, have a flair for novelty, a solid knowledge of his equipment and lots of imagination.

A press photographer's salary ranges upwards from $10,000 to $12,000 a year.

Inside a gymnasium, following the action, at 1/60 sec., f/4.

138 What are the job opportunities in Canadian cities for a recent photography graduate?

I would hope that you never stop studying, learning and perfecting your technique just because you have completed a basic photography course. The real professional keeps developing and tries to stay abreast of the latest technical innovations.

In one sense young Canadian photographers have a distinct advantage. There is no professional body which regulates this trade, as there is for, say, electricians or plumbers. If there were one, the young photography graduate would have to undergo an apprenticeship of three or four years before being able to "practice" as a full-fledged professional. He would have to conform to a body of rules or code of ethics. However, as a photographer, anyone is free to practice his calling and to choose his own specialty. The possibilities are endless.

Today, photography plays a role in almost every sphere of activity in the world of work. No matter what your business, you are bound to have some contact with photography, directly or indirectly. Nevertheless, the economics of trade in a large Canadian city will only make room for about 75 new photographers and 25 new lab technicians each year, in terms of full-time work. But be assured that your chances of being able to work are very good, assuming you really want to work and that you are **persevering.**

The following list represents only a fraction of the entire range of special fields in which a young photographer can get his start:

Medical photography, industrial photography, commercial photography, photo-journalism, fashion photography, catalogue photography, child portraiture, wedding photography, display photography, animal photography, macrophotography, still photography for the cinema, postcard photography, sports photography, public relations photography, advertising photography, landscape photography, nude photography, microphotography, photo retouching, studio photography, lab work, convention photography, calendar photography, legal photography, infant photography, family photography, magazine photography, TV photography, illustration photography for art directors, aerial photography, underwater photography, assistant to a professional photographer, photography for travel agencies, flower photography, ID and passport photography, human interest photography, racehorse photography, photography of art objects, scientific photography, meteorological photography, astronomical photography, adult portraiture, still life photography, 3-dimensional photography, art photography, photography for the armed forces and so on over an almost limitless range.

139 Do you think that chance plays a part in getting a really superb photograph?

"Being lucky" in regard to taking pictures always strikes me as an odd concept. Luck to me is like throwing the dice several times in a row and hitting seven every time.

Luck is only one factor among many and one on which you can never count. The serious photographer relies on his experience, his intuition, his awareness, his constant readiness and an eye which is trained to pick out things that the next person would never notice. "Luck" in other words, is simply a certain way of working, backed up by an innate ability to anticipate just about anything.

To say a champion racing driver is lucky because he comes in first is a little too easy. It overlooks his daring, his cool nerve, his reflexes. The photographer who knows how to pick the time and place for his shot, and is prepared to wait patiently, will undoubtedly be rewarded.

I must confess that some of my own photographs are catalogued as "lucky". But if the number of these photos is very large, perhaps we should look for another explanation. The process of finding an exceptional image is very systematic and is the result of long experience and a constant desire to improve one's work. Good luck anyway!

140 Is it possible to earn a living by working in such a specialized field as architectural photography?

I am one of those people who believe firmly in specialization. This statement is perhaps unusual coming from a press photographer, who is usually considered a jack-of-all-trades in photography!

If I had to choose one particular field in which to work I would choose architectural photography without a moment's hesitation.

This is not a field which demands great imagination. On the other hand, it does require great technical polish. It usually calls for the use of large format cameras with special capabilities for architectural work.

The architectural photographer must develop an eye for shapes, masses and perspectives. He must also be patient enough to wait for the moment when the light is just right.

These photographers often work hand in hand with architects, but their scope is not limited. Once you get your start, a world of possibilities for selling your work opens up. All the firms and individuals who have participated in putting up a building — the engineers, the contractors, the suppliers — will be interested in your photographs for use in their own promotion or publicity.

Architectural photography is an exciting and well paid line of work. An experienced architectural photographer can quite easily command $100 to $200 a day as his basic rate, for a dozen black & white interior and exterior photographs.

The use of 35mm in architectural photography is fairly rare — understandably so. Nevertheless, with a little "luck", it **is** possible to take a first prize for all of Canada with a 35mm camera.

st B&W Architectural/Antoine Desilets,
ntreal.

141

I like to shoot a particular subject in a number of different ways, but after five or six shots I often find myself running out of ideas. What can I do to stimulate my imagination

This is an important question! The day people realize that a good photograph is 95% imagination and 5% technique, we will have taken a great leap forward in the art of photography. Creativity and imagination are obviously indispensable elements for a career in photography. If many people lack imagination, I think it is because their situation or their work does not demand that they develop their imagination. Generally, people only do what they have to do. When it becomes necessary for them to exercise their imagination, it is amazing how often they will rise to the occasion.

Developing your imagination is much like the process of learning a foreign language. Once you start to master a language, you must keep speaking it. Your imagination is like a fire burning away in your mind which must be fed with a variety of visual and emotional stimulants. Develop your sensibilities until you become supersensitive! I know some brilliant photographers but they do not work like geniuses all the time. They become inspired for a time and produce some exceptional photographs. It happens to everybody, and it will happen to you too. (See Question 140)

If your favorite exercise is thematic photography or variations on a theme, I strongly encourage you to continue because this is probably the best kind of visual experience you can get. It is a very liberating form of work, and there is no excuse for feeling unimaginative after just five or six photos ... that's hardly a beginning. You should begin to feel low on ideas after twenty-five or fifty photos. This is the kind of challenge you have to keep facing regularly. A thematic project does not have to be completed in three or four days. As an example, I have been at work on a particular photographic study for over four years. I must have about 150 photographs of Quebec bell-towers, each more interesting than the last. Subject-matter like this is inexhaustible. I have another project involving three particular urban landscapes. Every time I pass by one of them, I try to discover something new. I find it quite a challenge, especially because the subjects are quite im-movable.

Begin with a smaller more man-ageable subject. Take everyday objects like an alarm clock or a cup and saucer and put them into bizare and unexpected sur-roundings. Open the door wide to fresh experiences. Come on, get out there and create!

If you are looking for a really good view... a helicopter is the answer.

Seeing without being seen.

142 Are there penalties under the law if a photograph is published without permission?

In North America, anyone who is involved in a fire, a crime, an accident or any other public event cannot prevent his photograph from being published in a magazine or newspaper.

This is reasonable or else we would never see any photographs in our newspapers; it is impossible for photographers to obtain clearance from all these people.

A photographer has the right to photograph politicians, kings, queens, princes, princesses, actors, actresses, and all public personalities. What is more to the point is how you use the photograph.

No photograph can be used for any **advertising purposes** without the consent of the person involved.

The important thing is not to miss the opportunity for a good photograph. You can always shoot first and ask questions later!

If a photograph is published, the responsibility always rests with the editor, not the photographer. Generally speaking, people do not object to having their picture published in a magazine or newspaper. Indeed, if they are not made to look ridiculous and their reputation of integrity is not damaged, many people will be more than co-operative. In the final analysis it is a matter of common sense.

Avoid taking photographs which amount to an invasion of the subject's privacy. You may save a lot of trouble by getting a release signed, especially if you have taken a photograph of someone who is not accustomed to publicity.

Disputes which involve invasion of privacy are usually settled out of court, but don't take any chances. You will find a sample release form on the opposite page which you should use if you have any doubts.

DATE:

PLACE:

DESCRIPTION OF PHOTO:

              I, the undersigned, consent to the use of this photograph for publication in a magazine or newspaper, or for promotional purposes.
              As parent or gardian of the child appearing in this photograph, I, the undersigned, agree to let the maker of this (these) photograh(s) use it (them) as he sees fit, providing he consults me on the matter beforehand.

SIGNED:

143 Why are good photography clubs so hard to find?

It is quite natural for amateur photographers to want to get together and exchange ideas. I know that a number of business firms have started such clubs, but they are generally reserved for their own employees. Similarly, clubs in colleges and universities are run by and for the students.

Even with all the contacts I make while at work, I have been unable to get in touch with any club in my own area. I think there are probably more community-oriented clubs of this kind in suburban and rural areas.

Why not get together with three or four friends and share the cost of an expensive piece of equipment, like a Seal mounting press, or share the cost of setting up a darkroom — if you can stay out of each other's hair long enough to get your own work done!

Man in search of photography club. . .

144   Do you ever allow anyone to come along with you on an assignment and watch you in action?

I wonder how many times I have been asked this question! While flattering to the professional photographer, it is the sort of question which can really put him on the spot.

Is there really such a great difference between a professional photographer and any other? Most of us use the same equipment. To see a group of press photographers all working in the same place, you would think their pictures were all going to turn out the same, because they seem to be shot from the same angles at about the same time. Yet there will always be one or two among them who will quietly find a way to shoot something more unusual. They will probably have stepped away from the group, in order to get their shot through a hole, or from behind the subject's back so that they take in the battery of other photographers. Anyone watching these movements back and forth will probably not be much the wiser about just what the photographer has in mind for his shot. Without getting his own eye on the viewfinder, he would have to get the professional to **think out loud.** What counts is what is going on in the photographer's head.

In other words, the photographer's actual behaviour on the job tells you very little about what he is really doing. I enjoy meeting photography enthusiasts when I am on assignment, but I doubt very much that anyone would learn much from watching me.

I think this picture tells you much more about the kind of atmosphere that prevails at an NHL draft session than the photo below, which is the sort always seen in the newspaper.

145 What is meant by the term "photogenic"?

Being photogenic does not necessarily mean being handsome or beautiful, although that helps. A portrait or fashion photographer might say of his model "She's very easy to photograph", because she can strike the required poses without difficulty and thus make their work as efficient as possible. Professional models must work this way. They never have any trouble finding their "good side" for the camera.

A photogenic person is able to face a movie or still camera and remain completely relaxed and unselfconscious. This is what is expected of professional models and actors. Even a good-looking face will not shoot well if it is tense or nervous. Someone who is said to have a winning smile is usually photogenic. Most children under the age of seven are very photogenic, simply because they are quite oblivious to what is going on when they are being photographed; they do not care if the finished product is flattering or not.

It is the responsibility of the photographer to use all the methods of his art to make an unphotogenic face a little less so. Sometimes a young photographer will mishandle the photogenic aspects of his subject by using a wide-angle or standard lens for shooting portraits. Portraits should always be shot with a lens of at least 85mm or longer. With the correct approach, you can make just about anyone photogenic!

Do you think she is photogenic?

146 I have just finished school and would like to study photography seriously. Can you give me any information concerning schools and courses?

∎ ■ ∎

Depending on where you live and would like to study, there are several alternatives open to you. You can enroll in a private course of instruction such as those available through various Applied Arts Academies or Schools of Photography. You can also attend classes or take courses for credit at Community Colleges, Institutes of Technology or Technical Schools.

At private schools your tuition fees may be significant (about $500) but they tend to allow students to choose the times for their instruction (morning, afternoon or evening). You do not, therefore, have to be a full-time student. You can be employed at least part-time during the day. At private schools students can usually enroll at any time during the year. A full course usually lasts for six months.

Public institutions such as Community Colleges and Technical Institutes usually have only modest tuition fees but require attendance at classes at specific times. Attendance is often limited, but facilities are very good.

Both sorts of training institutions make some effort to place their graduates in suitable job positions.

147 Although photographic equipment is so fragile, is it possible to use the equipment heavily and yet make it last a long time?

If people really learned how to take care of their equipment, the repair business would slowly disappear and there would be many unemployed technicians. However, I do not think this is about to happen.

First, you should use a new camera empty a number of times before shooting with it. The moving parts and the lubricant also need to be loosened up after a long period of storage. You should try out all the shutter speeds a number of times.

Any parts where metal rubs on metal and where there is a risk of wear should be oiled from time to time (see photos opposite).

Never, never attempt to lubricate any part of the diaphragm, the shutter or the film-winding mechanism. This delicate work must be left to an expert. All you need do is consult the instructions that come with the camera: they will tell you exactly what to lubricate and what not to lubricate, what oil to use and how to do it.

Dust has a tendency to soak up oil. It is therefore important to dust your camera (and all your photographic equipment) carefully and regularly.

Occasionally, a tiny screw will work itself loose from the lens. You will need an assortment of miniature screw drivers to keep them all tight. You may want to keep them in place with a drop of clear nail polish after you have tightened them.

The worst elements of all for your camera are water and sand.

The best way to make sure your equipment keeps functioning is to have your camera(s) checked regularly by someone who specializes in the maintenance of cameras and other photographic equipment. Do not wait for something to go wrong. "Preventative maintenance" is essential.

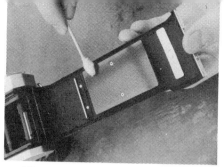

The pressure plate often harbours small impurities that may scratch the film.

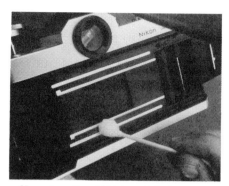

Keeping the inside of the camera clean is as important as keeping the lens clean.

When you finish shooting, always replace the lens cap.

Unless you happen to be a press photographer, you should always use a case.

Always clean the lens with Kodak Lens Cleaning Tissue. Use a handkerchief or tie only in emergencies. . .

148 Can you give a brief chronological outline of the history of photography?

Photography, as we know it, is a mere 150 years old. However, the ideas and principles are not new. It is useful to look back over the years and note some of the main contributors to the development of the art.

1521: Leonardo da Vinci talks about the "camera obscura" principle for making drawings.

1568: Daniello Barbaro perfects a lens for the "camera obscura".

1588: Battista Della Porta describes the "camera obscura" further and uses it for observing eclipses.

1725: Johann Heinrich Schulze proves that silver salts darken when exposed to light.

1793: The "camera obscura" becomes a "physionotrace". This device produces a copper engraving from which a number of prints can be made.

1802: Tom Wedgwood uses a "camera obscura" to fix an image on a silver nitrate plate.

1816: Nicephore Niepce produces a few poor quality "negatives" on paper. They do not last because he has no fixer.

1826: Niepce gets his first "permanent" photo by a process called "photogravure".

1829: Niepce works with Jacques Daguerre in order to improve his process; the result is the "daguerreotype".

1837: Daguerre is satisfied with the permanence of the image on his film.

1839: W.H. Fox Talbot perfects the first emulsified paper which allows a series of "positive prints to be made from a negative (known as a "talbotype").

1848: David Octavius Hill is generally recognized to be the first great portrait photographer.

1851: Frederick Scott Archer perfects a "collodion" emulsion which can be spread on a glass plate. However, it must be exposed before drying. From now on film will be perfectly flat.

1860: The birth of documentary photography and stereoscopy. Film speeds increase to permit exposures of about 1/25 sec.

1880: The modern age of photography begins with the appearance of ultra-sensitive emulsions made of silver bromides.

1885 to modern times: The popularity of photography spreads and gives rise to a spectacular application of creative energy, in both the manufacture of photographic equipment and the pursuit of photographic communication. By the year 2000 photography may have become the universal language.

Question: What is imagination?

Answer: A mental faculty that creates new images by combining ideas etc, etc.

books

*A New Series of General Trade
Paperbacks by Canadian Authors
Published in Canada*

EXCLUSIVE DISTRIBUTOR:
COLLIER-MACMILLAN CANADA, LTD.
SERVICE AND DISTRIBUTION CENTRE
*539 Collier-Macmillan Drive
Cambridge, Ontario N1R 5W9
Tel. (416) 449-7115 / (519) 621-2440*

*Printed by
IMPRIMERIE ELECTRA*

A GUIDE TO SELF-DEFENSE

Louis Arpin

This book is intended for men and women who are not necessarily sportsmen or athletes, but who want to know to defend themselves in an emergency.

304 pages,
Fully illustrated

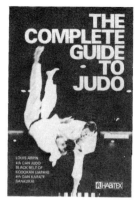

THE COMPLETE GUIDE TO JUDO

Louis Arpin

Beginning with the origins of the Martial Art known as the Way of Gentleness and proceeding through all the Ground and Standing techniques, this carefully written handbook will be invaluable to anyone interested in the sport.

Fully illustrated
262 pages

SANKUKAI KARATE

Me Yoshinao Nanbu

Karate is a system of defense using no weapons — only feet, knees, elbows, fists, edges of the hands and fingertips. Sankukai karate is a form which uses many techniques developed by the author, Me Yoshinao Nanbu.

Fully illustrated
235 pages

AIKIDO

Text: M. N. di Villadorata
Photos: P. Grisard

Until 1945 Aikido was "reserved" by the elite Japanese military establishment as its special form of self defense. It is a system of attack and defense where one or both participants are armed with staffs, spears, swords or knives.

Fully illustrated
220 pages

KUNG-FU: KARATE SAMURAI STYLE

Roger Lesourd

The author briefly traces the origins and evolution of this martial art and shows, with the help of approximately 400 photographs, the fundamental positions, and the basic and advanced katas.
256 pages, illustrated

JOGGING

Richard Chevalier

The author, a teacher of physical education, recommends how you can maintain or acquire good physical condition through jogging. How to run; how to breathe; how to dress; the effects of jogging on physical condition.
232 pages, illustrated

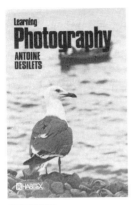

LEARNING PHOTOGRAPHY

Antoine Desilets

This book provides instruction on proper camera use, including many tricks of the professional, and essential information on developing and printing film, enlarging, and special effects.

224 pages, illustrated

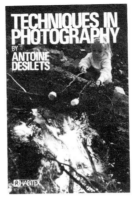

TECHNIQUES IN PHOTOGRAPHY

Antoine Desilets,

An invaluable handbook for every one interested in photography — amateur and experienced alike.

262 pages, Fully illustrated with photos, charts and diagrams

TAKING PHOTOGRAPHS

*Antoine Desilets
in collaboration with
Roland Weber*

A complete guide to taking photographs, covering such topics as Apparatus, Filters, Film, Light Meters, Flash Lighting, Viewpoint, Portraits and dozens of others.

*Fully illustrated
265 pages*

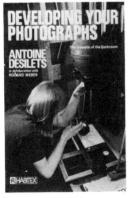

DEVELOPING YOUR PHOTOGRAPHS

*Antoine Desilets
in collaboration with
Roland Weber*

Everything you need to know about developing your own films, from choosing basic equipment through enlarging to special effects. A question and answer technique deals with specific questions in detail.

*Fully illustrated, colour plates
335 pages*

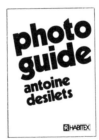

PHOTO GUIDE

Antoine Desilets

This simple guide provides a handy reference to the basics of still photography.

*Fully illustrated
45 pages*

SUPER 8 CINE GUIDE

André Lafrance

A technical guide to super 8 photography, designed for use by the amateur as well as the professional.

*Fully illustrated
55 pages*

WAITING FOR YOUR CHILD

Yvette Pratte-Marchessault

From the first signs of pregnancy to a complete course of postnatal exercises, this straightforward and informative new book provides the answers to the many questions a new mother may ask.

192 pages, Fully illustrated with photographs and drawings

PSYCHOMOTOR DEVELOPMENT IN THE CHILD

Didier Calvet

This clear, practical guide will help parents develop their child into a social being, enjoying life and becoming a part of the family more each day.

176 pages, illustrated

FEEDING YOUR CHILD

L. Lambert-Lagacé

A useful and valuable guide to preparing nutritious meals for very young children.

245 pages

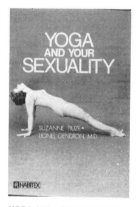

YOGA AND YOUR SEXUALITY

Suzanne Piuze and Lionel Gendron, M.D.

Two well-known authors combine their special knowledge and skills to describe a particular kind of mental and physical harmony — that of mind and sexual function. Physical function is explained, along with the principles of yoga as they apply to a healthy mind and body.

Fully illustrated 190 pages

INTERPRETING YOUR DREAMS

Louis Stanké

This fascinating new book, in a dictionary format, will help the reader understand the significance of his dreams and appreciate the activity of his subconscious.

176 pages

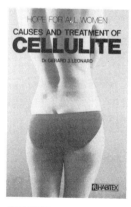

CELLULITE

Dr. Gérard J. Léonard

The author, one of the leading authorities on the subject in Canada, has written a book which will bring hope to all women who suffer from cellulite — hope founded on a scientifically based treatment which has been effective in reducing the problem.

224 pages, illustrated

WINE: A PRACTICAL GUIDE FOR CANADIANS

Pierre Petel

A remarkable little book — humourous as well as informative — written by a Canadian for Canadians in terms of wines available in Canada today.

176 pages, illustrated

FONDUES AND FLAMBÉS

Suzanne and Lucette Lapointe

Easy to read format presents the recipes clearly and concisely.

144 pages, illustrated

FISH AND SEAFOOD

Sister Berthe

200 delicious recipes for both daily and special occasion meals. This book also contains a chapter of practical explanations with useful illustrations showing how to open and clean fish.

216 pages, illustrated

A GUIDE TO HOME FREEZING

Suzanne Lapointe

This useful and comprehensive guide to the use of a home freezer is indispensable to anyone who plans ahead. Many ideas, recipes and suggestions are included.

184 pages

A GUIDE TO HOME CANNING

Sister Berthe

An extensive collection of recipes for canning and preserving — ranging from meats and fish through to jams and jellies.

264 pages

BLENDER RECIPES

Juliette Huot

A new collection of recipes and ideas for tasty and nutritious dishes which may be easily prepared using that most versatile kitchen tool — the blender.

174 pages

HELP YOURSELF

Psychotherapy Through Reason

Lucien Auger
This guide to self-understanding provides a clear and simple method for overcoming emotional troubles.

168 pages

LIVING IS SELLING

Jean-Marc Chaput
All the tricks of dynamic selling are revealed here by an experienced and successful salesman.

198 pages

8/SUPER 8/16

André Lafrance

Everything one might want to know about home movies, film making and film production is described in this handbook. It is intended primarily for the amateur, but is also an excellent reference for the more accomplished film-maker.

Illustrated
245 pages

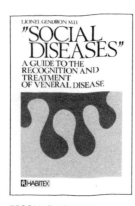

"SOCIAL" DISEASES

A Guide to the Recognition and Treatment of Venereal Disease

Dr. Lionel Gendron

—especially among the young. This book has been written so that the general reader may understand the causes, recognize the symptoms and appreciate the long-term effects of venereal disease.

122 pages,
Fully illustrated

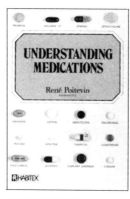

UNDERSTANDING MEDICATIONS

René Poitevin

What is a stimulant, a tranquillizer, a sedative, a vitamin or an amphatamine? How do they work? What are their effects? The author, a graduate pharmacist, answers these and many other important questions.

128 pages, Illustrated
in colour

MOZART SEEN THROUGH 50 MASTERPIECES

Paul Roussel

A fascinating account of Mozart's adult years and the circumstances surrounding the composition of 50 of his greatest works.

344 pages

CARING FOR YOUR LAWN

Paul Pouliot

The complete guide to the development and maintenance of a beautiful lawn. The author provides many useful tips on lawn care.

Fully illustrated
279 pages

GARDENING

Paul Pouliot

Everything the amateur gardener might want to know about gardening in Canada is contained in this outstanding book by a leading Canadian agriculturalist. Topics range from preparing the soil through bulbs, grasses, trees, house plants and plant protection. A Gardening Calendar is a special feature.

Illustrated
465 pages

TREES, SHRUBS AND HEDGES

Paul Pouliot

This illustrated guide provides the gardener with all the information necessary to plant, maintain and protect Canada's woody plants.
336 pages, illustrated

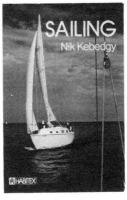

COMPLETE WOODSMAN

Paul Provencher

An invaluable handbook for the serious woodsman, this book is a basic guide to survival in the woods. It contains complete directions for every conceivable situation which might be encountered. A fascinating and useful handbook.

Fully illustrated with line drawings — 225 pages

SAILING

Nik Kebedgy

Not just a book for racers, *Sailing* describes some of the background of pleasure sailing and provides much valuable information about the more subtle aspects of the sport.

Fully illustrated
275 pages

VISUAL CHESS

Henri Tranquille

This book illustrates simple moves which occur in actual play and which are logical and easy to understand. Many celebrated attacks and defenses drawn from famous games are also included.

175 pages, illustrated
in two colours